Strategies for Studying

For successful studying after 16

CAREL PRESS

D0256155

Published by Carel Press Ltd
4 Hewson Street, Carlisle, CA2 5AU
Tel 01228 538928
Fax 591816

©1997 Mike Coles & Chas White
Revised edition 1999, reprinted 2000

Multiple Copies
Multiple copies of this book, for individual student use, and as an alternative to photocopying, may be purchased at a discount from the publishers.

Publication information
Illustrations: Craig Mitchell
Editor: Christine Shepherd
Cover designed by Arthur Proctor
Photos: Howard Barlow; Weald College, Harrow
Inside back cover photo: Neil McAllister

This is a completely revised, expanded & updated edition of a book first published by Collins.

Printed by MFP Ltd, Manchester

British Library
Cataloguing in Publication Data
Coles, M. (Michael)
Strategies for Studying: active approaches to study for success at A level, Highers, GNVQs.
1 Study Skills
I. Title II. White C.
371.30281

ISBN 1 872365 38 8

Environmental information
The book is printed on 100% recycled paper which is made entirely from printed waste, and is not re-bleached. Using recycled paper saves trees, water and energy, and reduces air pollution and landfill.

Authors

Mike Coles is a former Head of Science in a comprehensive school. He was Science Adviser for Suffolk, and then Professional Officer with the National Curriculum Council. He now works for the Qualifications and Curriculum Authority, as well as being a Research Fellow at the London Institute of Education. Until recently he was Chairman of Examiners for the Midland Exam Group. He is the author of several educational titles, including *Advanced Modular Sciences* (Collins) and *Active Science* which won the *Times Educational Supplement Schoolbook of the Year Award*.

Chas White studied at universities in both the UK and USA. He worked in a public library before becoming a school librarian and Head of Resources. He was subsequently Head of English in a comprehensive school. He is the author of a number of educational titles, as well as being co-editor of the acclaimed *Essential Articles* series.

Reviser: Bob Sapey
(University of Central Lancaster)

Additional sections
Making a video: Trish Jenkins
(London Film & Development Agency)

Talking your way through an interview:
Stan Barrett (author & broadcaster)

Using drama: Allan Owens
(author & lecturer, University College, Chester)

Revisers
Computer section: Maura O'Donoghue
(Deputy Head, Torquay)

Data section: Pippa Boot-Handford
(Ridge Danyers College, Cheadle)

Library & key reference resources: Sandy Foster
(School Librarian, Warwickshire)

Research: Stephen White
Additional work: Simon Thorp & Paula Stokes

Additional illustrations: D P Press

Contents

You can use these sidelines for your own notes and to respond to the ideas and suggestions in the book.

The sidelines also contain quotes from students and additional information.

Introduction

The fact that you're now reading this book suggests that you would like to find out how you could improve your study methods.

Study after sixteen is voluntary. You expect to consider subjects in greater depth, and you will be expected to work more independently. Many students, however, find difficulty in adapting to advanced study because they have acquired passive study habits.

Up to the age of sixteen you had to study and your teachers clearly directed the work. To take just one example, at school you probably experienced a great deal of note taking (copied and dictated notes) but not very much note making (arranging ideas for yourself).

This book is based on an extensive survey of students' approaches to study and many quotations from students appear in the text and in the sidelines.

Organising your learning is a special skill which not only helps you achieve success in examinations but is also appreciated in many jobs. Many employers and tutors consider this ability to improve your learning as a key skill. The skill is transferable from one situation to another.

You have already shown that you would like to become a better student. *Strategies for Studying* will show you the way to make progress and enjoy your studies more.

- Spend ten minutes now looking through the whole book to gain an impression of how you can become an active, independent learner.

- Then read the first two sections in detail, and complete the questionnaire in chapter 3 in order to focus on **your needs.**

1 Start here

Why should I change my study methods? I've already passed some exams, I know what suits me best.

Each person studies in her or his own way but many people will have acquired their study habits haphazardly. In this book you will learn about methods which students have found to be particularly effective.

I've had plenty of advice but it doesn't seem to work for me!

Yes, advice has its limitations, but this book offers more – it shows you how these learning techniques work. By trying the suggestions in this book you will be able to compare them to your present habits and to select the methods which suit you best.

Do I have to read the whole book through?

No. Read the next chapter (*Study after sixteen*, page 6), complete the questionnaire (page 9) and then choose which parts are going to meet your needs.

> *Don't compare yourself to other people. Compare yourself to the best you can do.*

SIDELINES & NOTES

2 Study after sixteen

'If I were starting my course again I would get myself organised.'

'If I were beginning again at college I would think more about preparing myself for a different type of study.'

> Spoon-feeding in the long run teaches us nothing but the shape of the spoon.
> E M Forster

Studying after sixteen is a completely different experience from before, partly because the material is more advanced, but also because you have to approach it in quite a new way – you are expected to take more responsibility for your own learning. Education is more of an adult partnership between teachers and students, in which you will need to organise your own individual approach to learning.

Students who are aware of this new approach are able to prepare for it and take it in their stride. For example, a traveller who knows her destination and arrival time can decide on the means and time of travel to suit herself. If, however, you set off and are not quite sure of where you are going, or when you have to be there, then it is easy to be sidetracked. At first you may enjoy the trip and its detours until you suddenly realise you have very little time left to travel a long way. Panic and last minute rush don't help, and you may find you've missed the boat.

'I would start working hard right from the beginning so that at the end I'd be confident of getting good grades instead of just hoping.'

Here are some comments by students on the differences between studying before they were 16 and studying after 16.
Note in the margin your reaction to these comments.
Which do you strongly agree (✔✔✔) or disagree with (✘✘✘)?

'Last year we were spoon-fed, i.e. by dictation.'

DICTATION

'It's difficult at first to use your initiative as previously in school you have always been told exactly what to do.'

'At college you don't just have to learn but you have to understand as well.'

'It can be more tedious and boring, perhaps because of the less varied course and the longer lessons.'

'You are left to study more on your own. You are not chased for work – if it is not done it's your problem.'

'Homework consists of lengthy essays and assignments rather than bitty questions to be given in the next day.'

'You are generally treated, often for the first time, as a responsible, mature person.'

'Unless it's what you're really interested in, the work can be mind-bendingly boring.'

'The work is much more analytical, and you have to think for yourself.'

'There's more discussion, with students giving their opinion, rather than being told everything by the teacher.'

'Learning skills, like information seeking and evaluation, are much more important now.'

'Now is the time when you can really benefit from using a computer effectively.'

'A quiet library is suddenly much more interesting!'

'Reading around the subject is now an important part of the course.'

'There's more work and pressure but also more freedom.'

'There is the impression that someone may be beginning to think about regarding you as nearly a person.'

'Nobody forces you to do the work.'

3 Are you satisfied with your study habits?

Whether you are naturally well-organised or not, you can raise your level of achievement by examining and improving your approach to study. Don't compare yourself to some kind of ideal student – they don't exist – but to the best you yourself can achieve. This means that you will be able to set realistic targets for yourself.

Read the questions below then circle the appropriate response.
✔ = Yes　　　✗ = No　　　? = Sometimes

Attitudes and approaches to study

1	Do you keep an aim in mind when studying?	✔ ✗ ?
2	Is the energy you put into your studies matched by the results you achieve?	✔ ✗ ?
3	Do you find it enjoyable to study?	✔ ✗ ?
4	Are you satisfied with your study habits?	✔ ✗ ?

(See chapter 7 Getting set for study)

Concentration

1	Do you find it difficult to make a start on your work?	✔ ✗ ?
2	Are you easily distracted from your studies?	✔ ✗ ?

(See chapters 8 Your body and your brain, 9 Study know-how)

Organisation

1	Do you know at what time of the day you work best?	✔ ✗
2	Do you set aside regular times for study each week?	✔ ✗ ?
3	Do you spread your study periods over the week?	✔ ✗ ?
4	Do you tackle the most important tasks first?	✔ ✗ ?
5	Do you take planned breaks?	✔ ✗ ?
6	Do you keep up to date with homework assignments?	✔ ✗ ?
7	Do you divide your time appropriately between your different subjects?	✔ ✗ ?
8	Have you got somewhere convenient to study?	✔ ✗
9	Do you waste time looking for pens and equipment, notes and files?	✔ ✗ ?

(See chapters 4 Organisation & planning, 5 Where to study)

Psychology of study

1	Do you reward yourself after finishing a task?	✔ ✗ ?
2	Do you know something about how learning happens?	✔ ✗ ?
3	Do you understand how memory works?	✔ ✗

(See chapters 7 Getting set for study, 8 Your body and your brain)

Libraries

1	Do you understand how a library works?	✔ ✗
2	Are you aware of all the services a library can offer you?	✔ ✗
3	Can you find information quickly?	✔ ✗ ?

(See chapters 12 Library and research skills, 13 Key reference resources)

Are you satisfied with your study habits?

Reading and books

1 Do you do any background reading for your subjects? ✔ ✘ ?
2 Do you find it takes you a long time to read a recommended book? ✔ ✘ ?
3 Do you read every book in exactly the same way? ✔ ✘
4 Do you understand how to use a dictionary and thesaurus properly? ✔ ✘ Partly

(See chapters 14 Book skills, 15 Reading, 17 Widening your vocabulary)

Notes

1 Are your notes easy to understand? ✔ ✘ ?
2 Are your notes easy to revise from? ✔ ✘ ?

(See chapters 9 Study know-how, 10 Making notes, 11 Abbreviations)

Assignments and Essays

1 Are your assignments/essays well planned? ✔ ✘ ?
2 Do you tend to repeat yourself in essays? ✔ ✘ ?
3 Do you tell the story of something instead of analysing the topic? ✔ ✘ ?
4 Can you distinguish between main ideas and supporting details or evidence? ✔ ✘ ?

(See chapters 16 Writing, 17 Widening your vocabulary)

Data

1 Can you interpret data accurately? ✔ ✘ ?
2 Can you create accurate charts and tables? ✔ ✘ ?

(See chapter 18 Dealing with data)

Computers

1 Are you familiar with the basic operations of the computer you use? ✔ ✘
2 Are you aware of its potential to help you in your studies? ✔ ✘ ?
3 Are you able to use

    a wordprocessor ✔ ✘ ?
    a database ✔ ✘ ?
    a spreadsheet ✔ ✘ ?
    e-mail ✔ ✘ ?
4 Can you make use of web sites which are relevant and helpful to your studies? ✔ ✘ ?

(See chapter 19 Computers)

Revision and exams

1 Do you leave revision until the last minute? ✔ ✘ ?
2 Do you panic at exam time? ✔ ✘ ?
3 Do you find it difficult to understand exam questions? ✔ ✘ ?
4 Do you run out of time in exams? ✔ ✘ ?

(See chapters 20 Revision, 21 Exam skills)

Analysing your strengths and weaknesses is the first step to improving your study habits.

Each individual will respond differently to this questionnaire.

Below are just three responses together with a comment about each.

Sarah

I feel a bit depressed. I don't seem to be doing anything right.

It is not a question of your study habits being wrong, but it is a fact that some techniques are more effective than others. If you experiment with the strategies outlined in this book you'll be able to choose those which suit you best, instead of simply using methods which you have acquired by chance.

Craig

IT'S CERTAINLY MADE ME THINK, MAINLY ABOUT THE IMPORTANCE OF ORGANISATION – I'VE ALWAYS TAKEN THINGS AS THEY COME UP TO NOW. ONE OR TWO THINGS, LIKE THE ESSAYS AND ASSIGNMENT SECTION, DON'T REALLY APPLY TO ME.

Being able to organise your time marks the transition from being a pupil to becoming a student. It is difficult, because as a pupil your teachers organised all your time in school and structured your homework. It's very easy to waste your free time.

Of course not all the sections in this book will apply to you. You don't have to read the book from beginning to end; instead decide which sections are useful for you and work on them.

Carol

I find it hard to complete this sort of self analysis - I suppose because it means I have to be self critical. Still this was useful - I'd like to find out more about the psychology of study and how to use a library. I sometimes waste ages looking in the wrong place in the library just because the assistants seem to be too busy to help me.

Don't think of it as self criticism, think of it as a way of analysing your habits so that you can improve them. Long established practices – habits – are difficult to break unless you see a very good reason for change. Learning something about the psychology of study may well suggest that you've more potential than you thought.

Self Assessment

Analyse below your own responses to the questionnaire.

. . . .

. . . .

. . . .

. . . .

. . . .

. . . .

. . . .

. . . .

. . . .

To help organise your thoughts you could use a SWOT analysis – Strengths, Weaknesses, Opportunities, Threats.

This is usually done using a grid:

Strengths	Weaknesses
Opportunities	Threats

Businesses also use this technique to improve their performance.

If you look at your responses to a section such as Libraries or Notes, you can put the **strengths** and **weaknesses** straight in the relevant boxes. It's important to know what you are good at, as well as knowing what you need to learn.

Next you need to think about the **opportunities** to help you learn - could you talk to a librarian or should you attend an induction session on note making?

Now think about what the **threats** are to you doing this – would you prefer to go home on time rather than attend an extra session? Do you believe that you can be taught to make notes?

Are you satisfied with your study habits?

This process can help you to be aware of **what** you need to learn, **how** you might learn it and what might get **in the way** of your learning. You can then decide how to approach the problems.

You may like to hear how someone else sums up your study habits. You could show your answers and your analysis to a friend and ask them what they think.

Friend's view

. . . .

. . . .

. . . .

. . . .

. . . .

. . . .

. . . .

4 Organisation and planning

Time tips

At college or school

'You have to learn to study in free time, and not waste it chatting. Get your priorities right.'

'I like to discuss work with a friend. It can be really helpful as long as we make sure we stick to the task.'

'Find somewhere quiet, like the library, where you can settle to your work.

At home

'Plan social activities after work but don't study on a Friday evening. Start afresh on a Saturday morning.'

'Don't set yourself goals which are impossible to reach.'

"Have one day off completely at the weekend. There is no need to become a recluse.'

'Try to work early in the evening so you can relax and rest your brain before going to bed.'

Organisation and planning

Do you agree with all these comments? Which advice is most important?

. . . .

. . . .

. . . .

. . . .

What conclusions have **you** reached about the best times for **you** to study?

. . . .

. . . .

. . . .

. . . .

Making the best use of your time

People work best at different times: for most the early morning is when they feel freshest, but some find that working late at night suits them.

In either case it is essential to see if you are making the best use of your time. A planner will help you to meet your study targets. First you must look at how you spend your time now. Fill in Study Week Planner I (page17) as accurately as possible. Leave out lectures and lessons but do put in

- private study and homework
- plans and commitments: e.g. sport, clubs, household jobs, a concert, a particular TV programme, meeting friends
- free time

Now you can see how much time you spend on each.

Complete this table

	Hours, minutes a week
Private study & homework	
Plans & commitments	
Free time	

Are you making the best use of your time?

RECORD SHEET

Study week planner 1: Your current pattern of study

	7-9am	9-11am	11am-1pm	1-3pm	3-5pm	5-7pm	7-9pm	9-11pm
SAT								
SUN								

	7-9am	9am-3pm		3-5pm	5-7pm	7-9pm	9-11pm
MON		Attending					
TUE							
WED							
THU							
FRI							

Organisation and planning

A study timetable
- **gives** you a target to aim for
- **spreads** your study throughout the week
- **helps** you to establish a routine for study so that you do not feel a conflict between study and relaxation time
- **encourages** you to keep up with the work. It is depressing to fall behind, and it is difficult to catch up
- **saves** time in decision making, and lets you get down to things

You learn best at the start and finish of a study session.

✔ Check off the points below as you plan your next week's study on Study Week Planner 2 (page 19).

Note things that you **must** do ☐

Plan at least 15 hours study over 7 days (More at exam time) ☐
- Making each study period a reasonable length ☐
- Planning a short break about every half hour ☐

Set definite times for starting and finishing your work ☐

Have something to look forward to after a study session meeting or phoning friends, watching TV or going out are all suitable rewards. ☐

Making a timetable every week would be a chore, but if you persevere for a few weeks then you will establish the habits of
- planning ahead
- using your time effectively

and these will become part of your approach to study.

After just a few weeks you will know your best times for study. Just one trap to avoid: don't let filling in the chart become an excuse for not getting down to work straight away. It might be best to fill in your planner for the next session at the end of each study session.

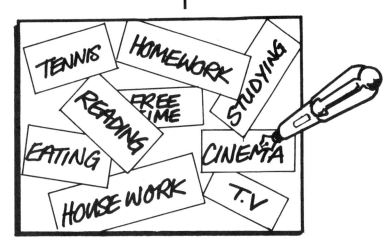

For an alternative viewpoint on planning and revision, see page 21 'Flush away those revision blues.'

RECORD SHEET

Study week planner 2: A future model for study

	7-9am	9-11am	11am-1pm	1-3pm	3-5pm	5-7pm	7-9pm	9-11pm
SAT								
SUN								

	7-9am	9am-3pm	3-5pm	5-7pm	7-9pm	9-11pm
MON		Attending				
TUE						
WED						
THU						
FRI						

Organisation and planning

Working on your own

'The work which has to be handed in earliest should be tackled first, even if it is the hardest.'

'A pile of work is often daunting when considered as a mass. Break it down into manageable chunks.'

'Do the hard things first, while you're still fresh.'

'The longer it's left the harder it is to do.'

'If you don't get into the habit of doing regular work at home you'll find it much harder to revise near exam time.'

CHECKLIST
English essay ✓
Van Gogh notes
Research Genetics
for General Studies
Read Othello 3 iii ✓
Watch 'What the
Papers Say'

'I find it a great help to make a list of the tasks I need to do, then put them in order and cross them off when I finish them. This way I can see I am getting somewhere.'

'Don't let it pile up.'

Do you disagree with any of these comments?

. . . .

. . . .

. . . .

. . . .

Summarise these comments in your own words:

. . . .

. . . .

. . . .

. . . .

Flush away those revision blues

Suddenly you've run out of legitimate excuses to avoid revising for exams, so here are 10 vital tips to put it off a little longer.

1   The first day. Make a horrendously complicated revision timetable. Copy it out several times using coloured Biros and shading. The key is to make the timetable as unrealistic as possible so it will need amendment at least once every two days.

2   Tidy folders and arrange work into labelled piles. This requires forward planning throughout the term so that notes are scattered around the room/house/city. If you are already organised, stand at the top of the stairs and drop folders over the banister, making sure all paper clips and staples are removed first. Your work should now be in messy heap at the bottom.

3   Plan to spend 45 minutes working and then have a 15-minute break. Bash watch against wall at start of break, talk to everyone you vaguely recognise and act surprised when you find you've been gone an hour.

4   Drink tea or coffee in abundance or take up heavy smoking. Tell yourself that you must have drink/cigarettes/sweets now or your brain will not function properly because it will be thinking about addiction. Repeat every 10 minutes.

5   Go to the library. Walk the long way, as fresh air will clear your head. If someone has sat in your regular seat by the time you arrive, abort all revision for the day. The working environment must be conducive to study, the wrong seat will ruin your concentration.

6   Hide reference books essential to the course somewhere near titles like Economic History Review 1964/5, so no one else can find them. Forget exactly where you put them and spend morning walking up and down aisles searching.

7   Ring mates from course at regular intervals to check on their progress. Meet at the pub to swap essays. Stay a while. Have panic attacks after speaking to hard-working, clever people and re-evaluate your need to have a degree, future plans and your whole personality. Using a housemate to cry on gives them a valuable excuse, deserting a needy friend for revision is unthinkable. Those in big houses who co-ordinate panic times could waste weeks.

8   Cook dinners quickly, thus giving yourself mild food poisoning. Alternatively eat a lot of curries, ensuring regular visits to the toilet.

9   Mention to the librarian that it seems silly to stock only two copies of the key text. Lean against counter and daydream as they ramble on about cutbacks, staff shortages and ungrateful students.

10 If all else fails, in the exam sniff, cough, flick hair, chew pen lid loudly. It's easy when you know how. Writing this has killed an hour or two for me. And isn't it my turn to clean the bathroom?

Emily McGarr, Sheffield University, from The Guardian

5 Where to study

> *Work in a library or a quiet room because you associate these places with study.*

Study environments

- Study the four sketches.
- List the most important advantages and disadvantages of each place of study.

Advantages

. . . .

. . . .

. . . .

. . . .

Disadvantages

. . . .

. . . .

. . . .

. . . .

Advantages

. . . .

. . . .

. . . .

. . . .

Disadvantages

. . . .

. . . .

. . . .

. . . .

Advantages

. . . .

. . . .

. . . .

. . . .

Disadvantages

. . . .

. . . .

. . . .

. . . .

Advantages

. . . .

. . . .

. . . .

. . . .

Disadvantages

. . . .

. . . .

. . . .

. . . .

Some people find it helpful to listen to music while they study alone, but it is important not to have the television or radio on, as this is distracting rather than helpful. It is also important to choose the right type of music – something that can put you in the mood for study and help you concentrate. But don't become dependent on music – you won't be able to listen to it in the exam.

What changes do you intend to make to your place of study ?

. . . .

. . . .

. . . .

. . . .

> *You learn best when you are relaxed and not distracted. Pleasant surroundings, without clutter, make a big difference.*

Have in the room your notes, books and a dictionary. Keep the room tidy so that you don't waste time looking for things.

CLEAR THE CLUTTER

If clutter is clogging up your study area or room, then it is also impeding all your studying. You will be wasting precious time simply clearing space to work and finding the things you need. Moreover, it will be the time at the beginning of a session when you are feeling fresh and are capable of learning best.

How clutter stops you studying

- You lose time searching for pens, notes, books.
- A cluttered desk or work area puts you off, a clear one invites you to study.
- You can't really use a few minutes for a brief study session if you have to clear the clutter first.
- Clutter makes you feel inefficient, guilty and depressed. It saps your energy.
- Clutter gives you an excuse not to start work.

How to clear the clutter

1 Make a point of clearing your desk once or twice a day. A clear desk at the end of the day – and therefore in the morning – feels especially good.

2 Only keep things you really need permanently on your desk.

3 Only keep things you genuinely need or genuinely like in your study area.

4 Deal with any stray piece of paper: act on it, file it or recycle it.

5 Get a large notebook or diary to use for reminders and lists. Don't use scraps of paper and backs of envelopes.

6 Sort through your notes regularly. Get rid of duplicates. The bonus is that you'll be reviewing your work as you do this.

7 Weed your notice board.

8 Remember you don't need to become obsessive about a tidy work area – you just need clear space for working and thinking.

9 Allow yourself regular time to de-clutter – it is time well spent.

10 Set up a 'just in case' box. If you have trouble throwing things away just in case you might need them, put them in a box. This gets them off your desk and off your mind. Sort through the box every few weeks. You will find you can throw things away more easily when you have proved to yourself that they are not needed.

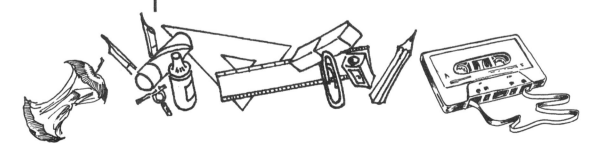

6 Wise up in lessons

Be there! Attendance is the first stage to success. Avoidable absence undermines your progress. You will miss vital explanations and quickly lose the thread of what you are studying.

Be prepared. This means not only pens, notebook etc – but also mental preparation. You will get twice as much from a lesson if you've reviewed the notes from the last lesson and done homework and any background reading. This is like an athlete warming up before a race – it gives you a flying start.

Make time. Make sure that you don't arrange to be doing something else immediately before or after a lesson or lecture so that you can arrive fresh and have time afterwards for organising and writing up your notes. Make a set time during the week to do your preparation, then it won't interfere with your social life.

Get involved. Sit at the front close to the teacher/lecturer. This will make you feel more involved, and you'll take more in. You'll be able to see everything clearly and you should be well away from possible distractions.

Participate. Ask and answer questions. This is the essence of learning, and is like personal tuition. Teachers always respond well to students who are keen and enthusiastic about the subject. Your enthusiasm will encourage the teacher's own enthusiasm.

Ask for more. If there's a little time at the end of a lesson teachers are often flattered to talk more about the topic, sometimes looking at its wider implications, or relations to other things. This helps to give you the big picture. Ask if there are any particular books, TV programmes or software that the teacher thinks would be useful to you.

Follow-up. After the lesson write up your notes immediately, rather than stuffing them somewhere out of sight. Do the necessary reading and start, or at least make a plan about, the homework.

Get into good habits then they will stick with you.

Think about the essential things that you learnt early in your life – learning to speak, for example. You learnt those things by doing, hearing, copying, watching, in a context of total involvement over a long period of time. Formal education is inevitably severely reduced in many cases to just listening and reading. Therefore you need to redress the balance and to make your learning experience as rich as possible.

SIDELINES & NOTES

❛Get up telling yourself you're going to enjoy the day.❜

❛Think about what you hope to achieve.❜

❛Experience is the name we give to our mistakes. Oscar Wilde.❜

❛A bit of well earned praise works wonders.❜

7 Getting set for study

Are you ready for success?

A strong, positive view of your studies and your chances of success will be a dominant factor in fulfilling your goals. Your hopes control a mental framework which remains with you whenever you study. Positive thinkers have a stronger framework to support them when they work. Students who are optimistic about their future and their ability to overcome the next hurdle in their study will be more aware of their strengths than their weaknesses. Appreciating your strengths will lead to greater confidence and then further success.

Of course everyone makes mistakes, but learning from mistakes is essential. A confident learner will face those mistakes and use them more effectively than someone who becomes depressed by them and feels that all effort is worthless.

Mental images

You can learn how to develop a strong mental image of yourself and your chances of success by:

1 Studying how other people prepare themselves

2 Organising your study method

You will have noticed how persistent and widespread your mental awareness is after you have bought a distinctive item, for example an article of clothing or a computer. You begin to notice all the similar items owned by other people. Every other computer is a Mac, every other person is wearing your style or colour of coat. Psychologists call this mental orientation: **set**.

Sports people will call it 'psyching'. Watch a high jumper or weight lifter before an event. Consider what goes through the mind of a tennis player during a break.

To have the confidence to score a goal, to believe you can score a goal, indeed, to have a mental picture of yourself scoring a goal, is a key preparation if you take your sport seriously. Imagine your chances of success if you started a race convinced you would come last!

' *A clear image of success is a stimulus to motivation.* '

Some mental barriers have proved very difficult to overcome. For example, before the four minute record for running the mile was broken, times were steadily improving:

1913	Jones	4 mins 14 secs
1915	Taber	4 mins 12.6 secs
1923	Nurmi	4 mins 10.4 secs
1931	Ladoumègue	4 mins 9.2 secs
1933	Lovelock	4 mins 7.6 secs
1934	Cunning	4 mins 6.8 secs
1942	Wooderson	4 mins 6.4 secs
1942	Haag	4 mins 4.6 secs
1942	Anderson	4 mins 2.6 secs
1942	Anderson	4 mins 1.6 secs
1945	Haag	4 mins 1.3 secs

But it was another nine years before the four minute barrier was broken. Could it have been that nobody believed it could be done?

1954	Bannister	3 mins 59.4 secs

A very short time after Bannister's record was set, Landy broke it:

1954	Landy	3 mins 58 secs

In 1955 Tabori, Chataway and Hewson all ran the mile in less than four minutes in one race! It seems a barrier had been removed. The present record is:

1993	Morceli	3 mins 44.4 secs

A Russian weight lifter only broke the 500 lb barrier after the scales had been rigged to deceive him by showing 499 lbs. Others have broken his record since.

In education it is acknowledged that if pupils believe that they are not very bright, perhaps because they are assigned the title 'set 4' or 'bottom stream', they will work at this level. As these pupils work, their mental set makes them more aware of their failures than their successes. It might be the case that their teacher, knowing they are set 4, will look for a set 4 standard because of her or his own mental set.

Mental set can be positive or negative

Consider the influence of parents, who believe their child to be bright, on the child's own opinion. Think of the opposite case. If two children from different backgrounds, with varying parental expectations, are equally intelligent, which one is more likely to succeed?

How can we use this very strong mental attitude to our best advantage in study?

- You must have a clear view of your goals.
- You must know your long term purpose.
- You must recognise the smaller, intermediate steps on the way to your long term goal.

Imagine being interviewed by someone who doesn't know you. The interviewer is trying to find out **why you are studying your course.**

Read the questions below then answer them aloud. Perhaps you can record your answers and then play them back afterwards.

1 What course are you studying, where and to what level?
2 How far through the course are you? How long does it last?
3 How are you getting on? Tell me about your most successful work.
4 Where are you concentrating most of your efforts at the moment?
5 Are you up to date with your work? What is your next task?
6 Is there a work experience element to your course?
7 When are your final exams? What form do the exams take?
8 What use do you hope to make of the qualifications you receive?
9 What are your career ambitions?
10 Which question(s) have you found most difficult to answer? Why is this? What can you do about it?

> *When doing work that is fairly easy, music helps me to concentrate, but harder work demands silence.*

> *Make a list of the other things you have to do, e.g. ring friends, ironing, etc., and do them after studying.*

Work out a question about your goals which you have not been asked but which would have posed problems or even embarrassed you if this interview had been real.

. . . .

. . . .

. . . .

. . . .

. . . .

> *Try out new study methods early in your course – when you are not under pressure. You will soon find out what works best for you.*

Spend some time thinking before writing your answer.

. . . .

. . . .

. . . .

. . . .

. . . .

. . . .

> *Build on success - remember a learning experience at school or elsewhere, when everything went right for you. Can you analyse why it worked? Can you draw any conclusions?*

Set for study

It is useful to have a clear idea of what you hope to achieve in each study session: this clarifies your thoughts and prepares your mental set. By listing what you intend to do, you put yourself in the right frame of mind and are therefore less likely to be distracted.

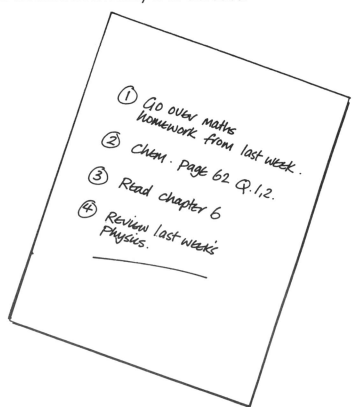

8 Your body and your brain

Mental abilities and age

What people remember most easily are outstanding things. These events are more likely to be outstanding earlier in our lives rather than later. We become familiar with the way things are in life; what is very unusual or special to a younger person will not be quite so special and memorable to a forty year old.

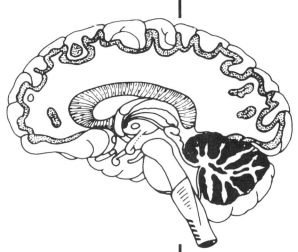

Mature students could hardly expect to do high quality work if their mental powers were forever decreasing. There is a decline in the number of brain cells as we age but this is insignificant compared to the vast number present. No theory of decline in mental abilities up to the age of 60 has been substantiated; in IQ tests no general fall in performance with age has been found. The brain and the thinking process become more specialised as more and more connections are made between brain cells. Experienced learners develop a more complex network of pathways through their brain cells.

Experiments on the protein content of brains of different ages have shown that protein levels increase with age. This is consistent with the idea of a chemical basis for memory and a steady increase in mental powers. Why then do some older people claim to be suffering from a declining memory? There are many reasons why a person of any age would claim this to be true, these reasons are examined on page 45.

A healthy brain

The brain requires 25% of our oxygen intake. The blood carrying this oxygen to the brain arrives via tubes of ever decreasing size until it reaches the capillaries in the cortex. As we get older these tubes stiffen, the apertures become 'silted up' with materials precipitating from the blood. Excessive intake of cholesterol, in foods containing animal fat, accelerates this deposition. It is likely that this process affects the circulation of the blood and can lead to the heart pumping at higher pressures. The supply of blood to the brain can be affected and there could be a reduction in mental effectiveness.

Take regular exercise

Exercise of the heart, lungs and blood system ensures a good, consistent supply of oxygen to the brain. Most people experience a strong feeling of well-being after exercise. Exercise relieves stress and improves circulation, leading to better mental performance. Students who take regular exercise do better than their sedentary colleagues.

Stimulation of your brain means using it well and often. The richer the environment, the more stimulating conversations, pastimes and entertainments you indulge in, the more effective your brain will be. People who have continued working into their eighties and nineties have shown little decline in their powers of observation, analysis and imagination.

Rest

During sleep the proteins which have been used up in the course of the day's mental activities are replenished. The brain can control the amount of sleep you require but a lack of sleep has serious implications for mental awareness and leads to stressful working. You need to be aware of the amount of sleep which seems to be right for you and make sure you manage at least that much.

Pacing your study

When you begin to study, the level of electrical activity within your brain rises. As some piece of new information is assimilated new electrical pathways through the brain cells are forged. The new pathways overlap with the pathways from older but similar ideas and information. These processes take time but the more pronounced they are the more likely you are to remember the information later.

Take breaks

A short pause to allow an adjustment to the new period of study will pay dividends in improved recall.

Consider what happens when you have finished. If you move on immediately to another subject there has been hardly any time for your brain to process the information and to establish its links with other related information. Indeed, if you proceed too quickly, new ideas will create interference which reduces recall later on. If a few minutes rest is taken after your period of study, a remarkable increase in appreciation of the study material occurs.

How often you take breaks depends on what you are studying. Routine arithmetic would require few breaks, say every 40 to 60 minutes. Studying a scientific concept or analysing a novel will require more breaks. After 20 minutes most people benefit from a short rest.

You will find that planning your study periods in this way will make your work more satisfying and give you a better appreciation of what you have achieved.

Your body and your brain

These two graphs show the difference in recall that taking breaks can generate.

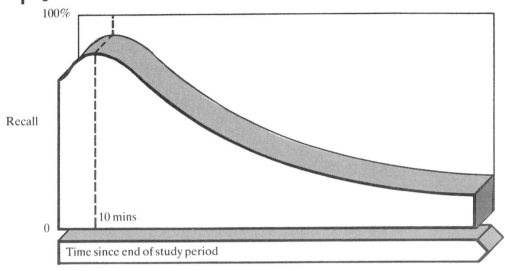

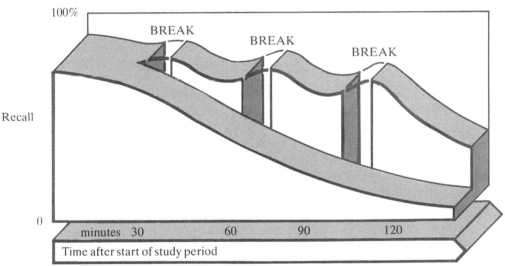

Beware of the temptation to continue without a break, sometimes the urge to keep going can be strong and easily rationalised. During a break try:

- moving away from your place of work
- taking some fresh air
- doing something routine
- letting your mind wander off the topic under study
- allowing yourself to relax

From what you have just read, say whether these statements are true or false:

- loss of brain cells leads to loss of memory
- the brain can be damaged by excess cholesterol
- exercise can make you a better student
- taking a break helps you to assimilate new information

The example on the next pages will give you the chance to practise the study techniques you have learned so far, while also extending your knowledge of how the brain works.

The brain: a study example

Imagine you are studying the brain. You would like to remember as much as possible about the structure of the brain and how things are stored in the memory. Study the text and the diagrams that follow. The references (A to E) are to the notes in the sidelines.

How your brain works

This unit will look at:

The structure of the brain

Using your brain

Brain cells

The synapse

Memory

The structure of the brain

The brain consumes a quarter of the oxygen we take into our blood to synthesise the protein required during thinking. The oxygen is supplied through membranes which surround the brain.[A]

A *Study the diagram carefully. Ask yourself which areas of the brain will be particularly involved in memory.*

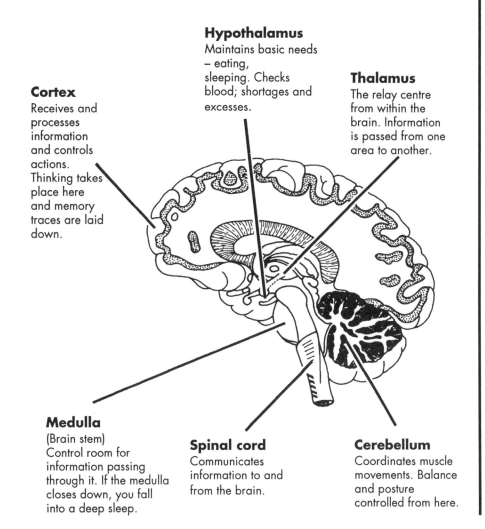

Hypothalamus
Maintains basic needs – eating, sleeping. Checks blood; shortages and excesses.

Thalamus
The relay centre from within the brain. Information is passed from one area to another.

Cortex
Receives and processes information and controls actions. Thinking takes place here and memory traces are laid down.

Medulla
(Brain stem) Control room for information passing through it. If the medulla closes down, you fall into a deep sleep.

Spinal cord
Communicates information to and from the brain.

Cerebellum
Coordinates muscle movements. Balance and posture controlled from here.

Your body and your brain

SIDELINES & NOTES

In the philosophy of artificial intelligence, John Searle has employed an idea called the Chinese Room. In this, he is locked into a room and people pass in pieces of paper with Chinese symbols on them. He understands none of this language and therefore understands nothing that he reads. However he has a book with a list of these symbols with further Chinese symbols that he must give as a response, which he does. Therefore to the people outside the room he appears to be able to give a meaningful response to their questions. The point is that he does not actually understand anything of the content of what he has done because he lacks knowledge. He is simply dealing with data and information. In effect he is operating like the CPU in a computer rather than as a person. This idea is intended to illustrate the difference between the human machine and a computer.

Searle, J.R. (1980) 'Minds, Brains and Programs', *Behavioural and Brain Sciences 3:417-24*

B *A short pause, to reflect on what you have read and to re-focus on the task, could pay dividends.*

Using your brain

Few students understand the basic functions of the brain or how to make the most of it. The notion that our brain functions like a computer is true only at the most basic level of comparison. A computer works in a linear fashion, and can call upon terrific resources of memory. The brain is capable of operating in a linear and multi-dimensional way as a continuous processor of information of many different types and sources.

Computers store data. This sentence, when stored in the memory of a computer, will actually be a series of 0s and 1s which in themselves are entirely meaningless. When these are fed into a word processing program, they are transformed into characters that appear on screen and can be edited or printed. At this stage they have become information. The difference with people is that they can transform that information into knowledge. The information is combined with much more information and used in a way that makes sense. The reason for this is that the information has meaning.

Our brain has the capacity to link streams of incoming information in a very complex way to produce a new impression of the information; in other words the brain can synthesise as it works.

Research indicates only 0.1% of our brain's capacity is used. There is also evidence to support the idea that we never forget; everything we ever experience is recorded in the brain.

Of course we cannot recall everything and it is important to distinguish between memory and remembering. If you were asked to name a few friends from your second year at school you could probably name one or two, and would then assume you had forgotten the rest. If a school photograph was produced some of the other names would spring to mind. Details like your classroom layout, and activities you were involved in, all help to re-establish your mental set and refresh your memory.

The brain thrives on use. A varied and rich environment, especially in the early years of life, considerably enhances the capacity for many operations. B

Brain cells

All our brain cells are with us when we are born. A tiny fraction of these cells die as we get older and are not replaced. However, we learn to use our brain more effectively as we get older and its capacity continues to increase. Since it is estimated that we use only 0.1% of our brain it would take a very rapid decay to affect our performance.

The cells in the brain are of two main types:
Neurones (nerve cells)
These are 'action' cells used for remembering, thinking, controlling organs and muscles. There are 10 billion of them.

Glia cells
There are ten times as many glia cells as neurones. These are packed between neurones and insulate them from one another. They also service the neurones, provide nourishment and remove waste. They hold the brain together.

Neurones

The dendrites of one neurone link to the end plates of other neurones forming a vast communications network. Information, in the form of electrical impulses and chemicals, travels down the axon and is relayed from neurone to neurone.[C]

SIDELINES & NOTES

[C] *Relate the information in the diagram to that in the text. You could copy the diagram and add the function of each part of the neurone to the appropriate label.*

dendrites   cell body   myelin sheath   end plates

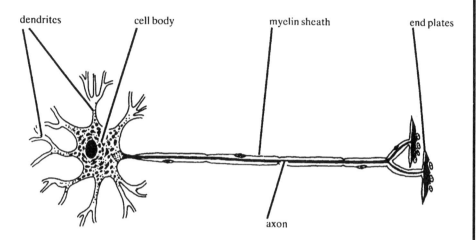

axon

As we experience things and learn, inter-neurone connections form, and the extent and complexity of the network is a measure of the development of the brain.

The synapse

A most important part of the system is the place where the end plates from one cell meet the dendrite from another. This 'connection' is called a synapse. Sometimes there is a direct electrical contact across the synapse but often there is not, and the minute gap between end plate and dendrite is the control over whether a pulse of information is passed between neurones.

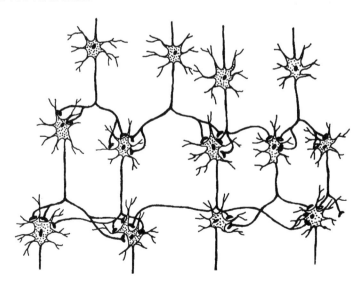

Your body and your brain

SIDELINES & NOTES

D *Are you clear about the function of a synapse? Could you label one on the diagram? Review this paragraph before you move on to more detailed information in the next.*

Each particular experience causes a specific trace of electrical activity through the network of neurones. Remembering this experience means reactivating this trace. The trace of electrical activity, the pattern of activated neurones, remains specific because some synapse junctions stop electricity flowing. The synapse is of obvious importance in thinking and memory. D

Memory

Large parts of the cortex become active when certain learning and remembering processes are taking place. At the same time there is appreciable protein synthesis.

When a neurone is activated by an electrical pulse, some chemicals, which are made in the cell body, move down the axon. It is these chemicals, which are proteins, that control the synapse. If certain chemicals are present at the synapse, the electrical impulse is passed on to the next neurone otherwise it terminates at the synapse. By this method an electrical pattern which results from some learning, can become permanently encoded onto the cortex. The electrical pattern which is the short term memory, is consolidated into a long term memory as a result of chemical changes at the synapse. E

When the memory is recalled, the encoded pathway is stimulated and the pattern of electrical activity recognised. By this theory we can appreciate the transient nature of short term memory.

E *You know that proteins created in the brain are important. Can you explain their role in long-term memory?*

There is experimental evidence from animal research that each memory or piece of learned behaviour has a specific chemical associated with it. These chemicals are also proteins and may encode a synapse. It has been possible to teach an animal certain behaviour and to extract and refine the chemical which was thought to have arisen from the learning. By transferring the chemical to the brain of another animal the behaviour was also transferred.

Test yourself

Could you explain to someone else what you have just learned? If you wish, you could use this list of key words to help you:

structure	computer
0.1%	cells
neurones	dendrites
axon	end plates
synapse	electrical activity
proteins	pattern
chemical changes	stimulus

9 Study know-how

SIDELINES & NOTES

A report from Canada (New England Journal of Medicine, 1997, 336 pp453-8) established that the risk of collision was four times higher when a driver was using a mobile phone and not therefore giving full attention to the road. In other words it's important to concentrate on one thing at a time.

Study your study

Your place of work should support your studies. For example it should have easy access to files, writing equipment and books for reference. It should be pleasant and interesting but away from distractions. Radio, television and conversation will demand your attention and break your train of thought.

SIDELINES & NOTES

❝ Improving your chances of remembering means making the strongest possible impression on your brain. ❞

Plan your work

Your work should be planned. You should have a clear idea of the purpose of your study (see pages 26 to 29). Planning evens out your work load and avoids overwork at key times. A steady work rate gives you time to reflect on what you have learnt and allows you to plan a pattern of review times (see pages 43-44). An important aspect of planning is producing a mental set (see page 26). Similarly, checking how you are doing with teachers, lecturers and tutors will lead to greater motivation and better study, especially if you use the Study Profile (page 39) to review your progress.

Breaks allow a full processing of information and improve recall (see pages 31-32).

Make it memorable

Try to ensure that the material you are learning is presented in an interesting, even striking, way. You can make your notes much more memorable by:

1 Organising them well, using sub-headings and showing links between different sections.
2 Designing them in a way which suits the mental processing which will follow. Make them clear, colourful and interesting, see Making notes, page 46. Pattern notes are a very useful variation (see page 40 for an example).

Knowledge is multi-dimensional so vary your study approaches - don't be narrow and one dimensional eg if you're learning Spanish, apart from attending classes try to
• watch any Spanish films on TV
• check if your library has any Spanish videos you can borrow
• read a Spanish newspaper or magazine
• listen to a cassette
• check out the latest computer software
• try the Internet for Spanish material
• get a Spanish book about a subject you are interested in
• make flash cards to paste round your room
• listen to Spanish records/CDs
• save up for a meal in a Spanish restaurant with Spanish waiters
• role play words or phrases ie do the action as you say the words
• learn a Spanish song

❝ You remember the unusual & forget the routine - novelty stimulates the brain. ❞

RECORD SHEET

Study profile: A self assessment

Regular reviewing of your progress will

★ keep you up to date   ★ raise your standards   ★ build on your strengths   ★ identify areas of concern   ★ demonstrate your progress

Term _____

Checklist

- achieving potential
- notes up-to-date
- homework done thoroughly
- acting on teachers' advice
- recommended reading
- practical reports up-to-date
- understanding of topics
- suitable notes for reviewing & revision
- background reading
- using resources appropriately
- interest and satisfaction

Subject				

Using the Checklist, comment on your progress. Be honest and realistic

Pattern note: Use your brain effectively

Link ideas

It is likely that our memories work by using extensive networks of brain cells. Each idea has its own pattern of cells but some ideas will have common cells in their patterns. You should be able to exploit this association to help you remember.

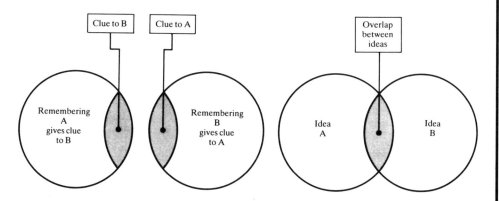

If you can forge links between well established ideas and new ones, then both the associated ideas become more strongly recorded in your memory. Give yourself time to appreciate how new ideas and existing ideas can be linked.

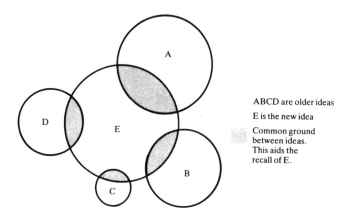

ABCD are older ideas

E is the new idea

Common ground between ideas. This aids the recall of E.

Look back at the text of *The brain: a study example*, page 33, and write down two firm links which you made between what you were reading and some information you already knew.

Link 1
New information:

. . . .

. . . .

Existing knowledge to which it was linked:

. . . .

. . . .

SIDELINES & NOTES

' Go over your notes now and again. It really helps you to remember them. '

Adult learning theory teaches us that it is important that learners are able to rehearse, practise and consolidate information. In other words when you first learn something, it will help if you try to use that information by applying it to a problem that will be useful to you. The process of application will help you to develop a better understanding of the information because you have been able to make it useful to yourself. If you have a better understanding, then you will find that you are able to remember it more easily because it becomes part of your knowledge. You may still have problems with remembering detailed formulae or the specific wording of important documents, but if you know what they mean and how to use them, you can always look them up.

Link 2
New information:

. . . .

. . . .

Existing knowledge to which it was linked:

. . . .

. . . .

Do the same for one link established when you looked at one of the diagrams about the brain (pages 33 and 35).
New information in diagram:

. . . .

. . . .

Existing knowledge to which it was linked:

. . . .

. . . .

Note down two points made in this book so far that have made a strong impression on your thinking.

1 . . . .

2 . . . .

How are these linked to your experiences?

. . . .

. . . .

Use your knowledge

Using new information or ideas probably strengthens the mental trace in your brain. Some ideas are readily applied to everyday life. For example, a science student who had just learned about the kinetic theory and the structure of substances, might think through the theory when boiling a kettle. Ideas which are difficult to associate with everyday events can be practised in some artificial way. Never underestimate the value of practice: pay serious attention to tasks, assignments and exercises that demand the use of newly learned information; do this using this six-point strategy:

1 **Recognise** the point of the task or question
2 **Research** the information required
3 **Design** a solution or answer
4 **Present** the solution or answer
5 **Appreciate** what you are learning
6 **Assess** your performance

Practise using your knowledge about how the brain works by answering these questions:

Some material is retained in long term memory and some is lost:

   a What chemical changes are significant in this process?

   b How are related facts linked in the brain?

Use the six point strategy to get the most from the exercise.

Teachers use questions as the first structured opportunity for students to review their notes.

Review your work

All newly learned information enters our short term memory. Unless the information is strongly associated with existing knowledge, or proves useful quickly, then it will be forgotten.

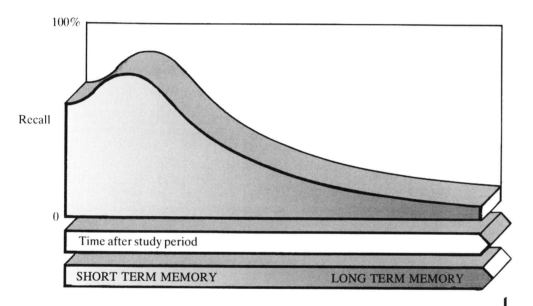

The long term memory develops as associations are appreciated either consciously or subconsciously in the days and nights that follow learning.

Recall improves immediately after learning stops. We can use this fact to improve our chances of remembering.

When a study session is finished it is worth taking a short break and then briefly going over the work again. This review means

1 **Looking** at the main points again
2 **Following** the logical progression of ideas
3 **Studying** your conclusions once more

Study know-how

The Forgetting Curve now takes this shape:

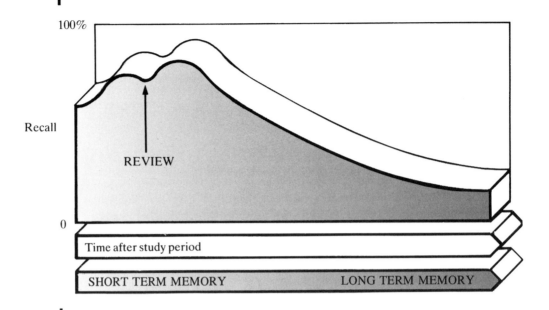

Notice how much more information is consolidated in the long term memory. Further reviews at intervals of a day, a week, a month and three months have a tremendous effect on the amount of information maintained in the long term memory.

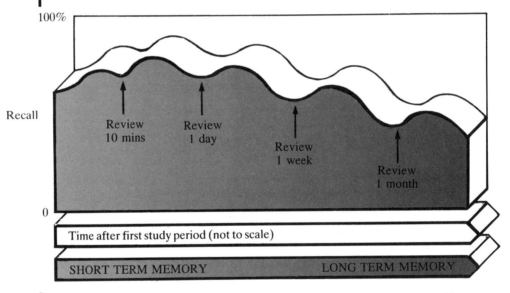

Reviewing and thoughtful note-making can have very significant effects on recall. Most students, however, do not review, because it requires organisation. Every day we would have to review yesterday's notes, and know what other notes to review. By using the Study Year Planner Wall Chart (Carel Press), however, and by making effective and memorable notes, only a few minutes will be required daily. In comparison to the hours you spend in study, a few minutes spent reviewing is an excellent investment.

Why do we forget?

Consider the theory that memory involves two stages:
Stage 1 Electrical activity which links up a network of brain cells, followed by **Stage 2** Chemical changes in the brain cells which make a more permanent memory trace.

The first stage is temporary and is therefore vulnerable. Reviewing can strengthen the electrical pathways and lead to a more accurate permanent memory. Without reviewing, the natural process of decay will reduce the chances of the second stage occurring. When this happens we forget things, and remember other things inaccurately.

We never learn things in isolation. During a study period new ideas overlap and interconnect with other existing ideas. If there is a weakness in a group of ideas, a misunderstanding or a misconception can spread to the associated ideas and weaken the chance of recalling them. For this reason, notes that you make should be accurate and, if necessary, quite detailed to avoid confusion.

' Don't struggle with a topic you don't understand, ask a friend or your teacher. '

Summary

Mental set can have a decisive influence on the quality of learning. When circumstances are right, when our mind is orientated towards a particular area of study, we can recall more. Reviewing work done in the previous session is an important starting point for study and should be built into your plans.

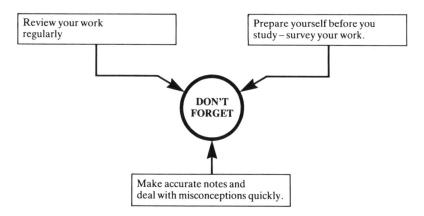

Surveying your plans will also pay dividends by creating a positive mental set. This is particularly important before examinations.

Learning my way

Jot down in the sidelines two or three things which describe ways of learning that really suit you. Use this chapter for tips.

Join a group of friends and compare your ways of learning. Are there ways that you should try out? Do people who are good at a subject learn in a different way from those who are not so good? Which are the best and worst possible methods for you?

10 Making notes

	Page
Compare these notes	46
Why make notes?	49
Copied and dictated notes	49
Key words	50
Sprays	51
Visual and pattern notes	52
Revising from notes	54
FACT SHEET: Filing notes	55
FACT SHEET: Storing notes: 1 & 2	56–57

❝ Make brief memory-jogging notes which can be expanded in essays. ❞

Compare these notes

Compare the following two pages of notes about Shakespeare's Theatre. List the most effective note making techniques.

. . . .

. . . .

. . . .

. . . .

. . . .

. . . .

❝ Write notes in point form with separate sub headings. I find this much easier than revising from long paragraphs and essays. ❞

Which set of notes would be most useful if you had to write an essay on this subject in an exam?

. . . .

. . . .

. . . .

. . . .

❝ Be concise – don't write down everything, as teachers always repeat themselves. ❞

Which set of notes is most like yours and in what ways?

. . . .

. . . .

. . . .

. . . .

. . . .

❝ Concentrate on the relevant points only. ❞

Shakespeare's Theatre   Craig S.

In 1598 the Globe theatre was built from the timbers of a dismantled playhouse called 'The Theatre'. The Globe was built by a theatre company called 'The Lord Chamberlain's Men' – Shakespeare was an important shareholder. Shakespeare was both an actor and a dramatist for the company: all his plays written from 1599 were performed at the Globe.

The Globe was burnt down on the 29 June 1613 during a performance of Henry VIII. A new Globe, with tiling instead of thatching, was built and opened on the 30 June 1614. The Globe was pulled down in 1644.

Performances were given during the afternoon. The auditorium was uncovered and surrounded the stage on three sides. People who stood here were called 'groundlings' – they paid 1d to get in. There were also three galleries. Members of the audience who sat on the stage itself were called 'gallants'. The Globe could hold up to 3,000 people.

Shakespeare's Plays

1590-91 Henry VI (3 parts)	1596 King John	1603 All's well that ends well
1592 Richard III	1597 The Merchant of Venice	Measure for Measure
Titus Andronicus	Henry IV Part 1	1604 Othello
1593 The Comedy of Errors	1598 Henry IV Part 2	1605 Timon of Athens
The Taming of the Shrew	The Merry Wives of Windsor	1606 King Lear
1594 Two Gentlemen of	1599 Henry V	Macbeth
Verona	Much Ado About Nothing	1607 Antony + Cleopatra
Love's Labour's Lost	Julius Caesar	Coriolanus
1595 Romeo and Juliet	1600 As You Like It	1609 Cymbeline
Richard II	Twelfth Night	1610 The Winter's Tale
1596 A Midsummer Night's	1601 Hamlet	1611 The Tempest
Dream	1602 Troilus and Cressida	1612 Henry VIII

SHAKESPEARE'S THEATRE   Carol A.

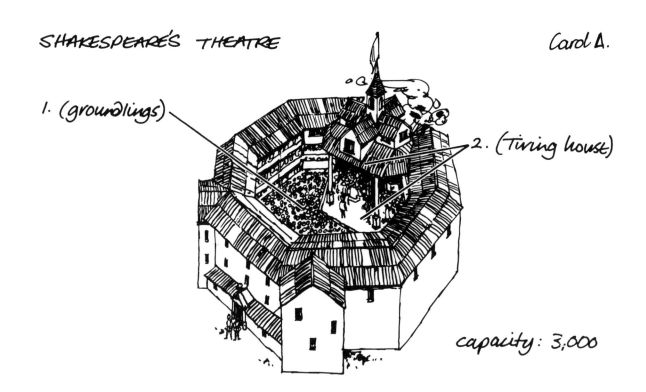

1. (groundlings)

2. (Tiring house)

capacity: 3,000

DEVELOPMENT • Pre 1575 no theatres. Performances: court, houses, halls, open air.
• 1575–1616 12 public theatres est in London (pop 200,000)
• 1598 Globe built by Lord Chamberlain's Men. Sh. a major shareholder.

ELIZABETHAN THEATRE	MODERN THEATRE UP TO 1960
1. Audience surround stage on 3 sides Daylight performance Mainly standing audience	Audience face proscenium arch. Sophisticated lighting. Seated audience.
2. Almost no scenery, no curtain No consistency in use of costume Soliloquy; blank verse; boy actors as women (till 1660)	Realistic scenery, stage curtain. Historically accurate costume Use of realistic effects Believable casting.
3. Doesn't confuse illusion with reality; ∴ encourages critical scrutiny, as well as enjoyment, of characters, themes + play.	Encourages dramatic illusion. Usually aims to be realistic and credible. A character's, not an actor's, stage.

Why make notes?

All students make notes but most do this without really thinking about why they are making them. Why should you make notes?

The palest ink is better than the sharpest memory. - Chinese proverb

1 Making notes makes you **concentrate** on what you are learning.
2 Notes help you **understand** because you put ideas into your own words and diagrams.
3 Notes **link** new knowledge to what you already know.
4 On paper it is easier to **distinguish** between important points and supporting details.
5 Notes are excellent for **revision**.
6 You **remember** things better when you have noted them down.

Copied and dictated notes

Notes which have been copied or dictated are a poor aid to understanding because you have missed the vital stage of interpreting the information for yourself. Therefore make sure you have understood what you've heard or read before you start to make your own notes.

Dictation goes through your ears, down your arm and onto the paper without stopping at the brain in between

If the teacher is using OHP transparencies, do not simply copy down what they have written on them. These are their notes and are often used to help them to remember what it is they are trying to teach. You need to make sense of the lesson for yourself and take notes that will help you to understand. Sometimes you may find the teacher's notes to be useful, but let that be a positive decision rather than assuming that you should always copy what s/he has written.

Notes can make very good sense at the time you take them but if you do not review them the same day you may forget what some of them mean. Rewrite your notes neatly or wordprocess them. Expand them so that things you put in your own shorthand at the time will mean something in six months time when you are revising for your exam. A good set of lecture notes will be as valuable as a good textbook.

Key words

Key words are the ones which are most loaded with meaning, the ones that unlock your memory. Key words are mostly nouns and verbs.

Read this article to discover what the writer feels are the dangers of relying on the Internet for educational information. Pick out the key words. See if you can find one sentence which summarises the whole article.

Dumbing us down

Convinced that kids will be left in the dust unless they get computer literate? Anxious about getting your local school wired up to the information age? Well, don't be. **Theodore Roszak** argues that computers in the classroom are not all they're cracked up to be.

By now most of what there is to say about the Internet is predictably clichéd. As usual it all has to do with stuffing lots of information into people's lives. Surfing the net, the hot new way to get information, begins by logging on to a variety of World Wide Web search engines like Yahoo that use keywords to find items. Almost all the search engines are commercially sponsored and feature advertising, some of it enticingly presented with lots of colours and blinking lights and cartoony images. Sometimes there is a prize for choosing this or that link, or maybe an Elvis Presley sighting is promised. Or there might be a big, bright link that says Don't Click Here! If you do you get a Dr Pepper soft-drink advert or some such.

Some Web sites are perfectly intelligent, conscientious efforts created by universities, government agencies, publishers or organisations like the Smithsonian Institution or the Library of Congress. Others feature celebrity gossip, sports, comics, jokes or pornography. With 20 or 30 machines running material like this in the classroom one can imagine teachers having some difficulty keeping everybody's attention focused on the assignment at hand.

If teachers can get the kids beyond the advertising and ask them to learn about, say, Aztecs, the search engine may produce in the order of 45,000 'hits' containing that word somewhere in the searched copy. This will include everything from soccer teams, used-tyre companies and disco clubs to bowling alleys and software firms... Yes, the search can be refined, but not always that easily for younger students since all the engines use different protocols. Even so, the refined search will continue to produce lots of wastage because the waste is there and because the search engine, simply keyed to words, is a dumb thing that cannot tell waste from value. On the Internet, there is no quality control as there would be in any school library. If a bibliography on the real, historical Aztecs surfaces amid the gleanings it may very well be out of date and unattributed. It might be the work of an amateur Aztec enthusiast in Peoria who never read basic materials in the field. If there is an essay on the Aztecs it may have been written by a fellow in Moose Jaw who has rather unusual theories about pre-Columbian peoples and space aliens. The Internet is a free-

for-all, as enjoyable as any conversation one might strike up in a saloon or coffee house. But it is hardly governed by the critical safeguards and intellectual structures that have been developed across the centuries to discriminate between honest thought and rampant eccentricity.

Some Web enthusiasts consider such structures a kind of elitist censorship. They might even regard the Dewey library catalogue system an infringement on the free flow of information. On the other hand I have heard no serious complaint that key words on the Web are now rented out by some search engines so that people seeking that kind of information will be steered toward a commercial product or service. On InfoSeek, a search for the words Christmas, Mothers Day, music, recipe (rented for as much as $1,000 each) is likely to produce some merchant's on-line catalogue.

Out of curiosity I recently asked a librarian if she had ever considered renting out space for advertisements in the card catalogue or its on-line version. She was first bewildered, then shocked. 'We would never do anything like that,' she said. That is the voice of public service.

In contrast, the Web is a creation of the entrepreneurial worldview. It favours high tech effects and attention-grabbing tricks. The key forces behind it are seeking desperately to transform the medium into the new television, the new movies. Their objective is to get millions to look at their site so that they can make a lot of money. This is no secret: the main, ongoing story about the Web is how much profit its backers are (or are not) making. What passes through the medium is bound to be shaped by those values, not by any significant regard for quality, truth or taste. Used as a teaching device the Web is an expensive way to distract attention and clutter the mind. I would not see it eliminated from our society for that reason, but neither would I choose it as an educational resource. Over the generations teachers have evolved skills to encourage a respect for quality, truth and good taste. I'm not sure I understand why we should, at the behest of entrepreneurial elements, now decide to retire those skills in favour of 'Yahooligans'.

Taken from an article in New Internationalist

Sprays

Sprays are a way of quickly jotting down all your ideas on a subject and linking them up. Sprays save time because you don't have to write sentences or put words down in any particular order.

Stage 1: Putting the ideas down

POLIO   TYPHOID

MEDICAL RESEARCH   CRUELTY

CIGARETTES

HUMAN   ANIMALS

BENEFITS   VIVISECTION

COSMETICS

ESSENTIAL   NOT ESSENTIAL

Stage 2: Making the links

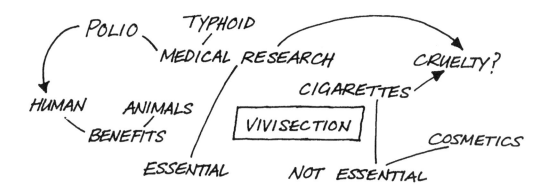

POLIO   TYPHOID
MEDICAL RESEARCH   CRUELTY?
CIGARETTES
HUMAN   ANIMALS
BENEFITS   VIVISECTION
COSMETICS
ESSENTIAL   NOT ESSENTIAL

1 Spend two minutes thinking about the problems faced by an old person you know.
2 Discuss the problems old people face with your friends. (Five minutes)
3 Make a spray about old age. (Ten minutes)

PROBLEMS
OF OLD AGE

Making notes

One picture is worth a thousand words.

' *Pattern notes are fun* '

' *Use flow diagrams to explain processes. Diagrams can omit half the written explanation.* '

Visual and pattern notes

Pattern notes (sometimes called 'mind maps') are a valuable supplement to ordinary written notes (called 'linear notes') because

- One pattern note can sum up many pages of written notes
- They make you concentrate on the fundamentals: the more relevant, an idea is, the closer it will be to the centre of the note
- They help you to see the relationships between aspects of a subject
- They link existing and new knowledge
- They put a topic into perspective
- Making a pattern note is a very active form of learning
- Every pattern note is different
- Because our visual memory is better than our verbal memory, pattern notes are a great aid to recall
- Colour and illustration stimulate the memory
- Pattern notes are an effective way of planning an essay
- They are an absorbing and fruitful method of revising
- Pattern notes are flexible because you can easily add to them

Look at the flow chart on aluminium below, and the pattern note on accent opposite. Now make your own pattern note or flow chart on a topic. Use colour-coding on related ideas; and print, box or underline headings.

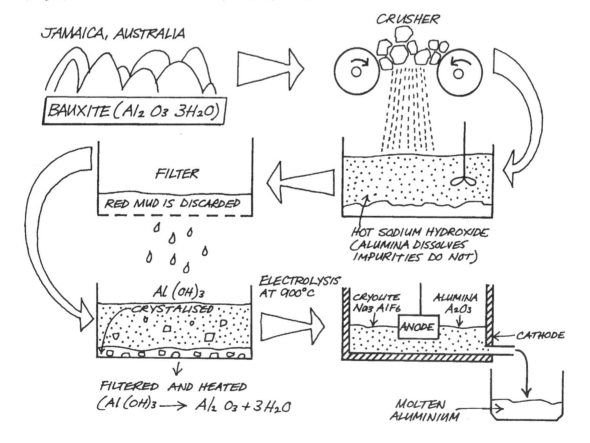

THE EXTRACTION OF ALUMINIUM

JAMAICA, AUSTRALIA

CRUSHER

BAUXITE ($Al_2 O_3 3H_2O$)

FILTER

RED MUD IS DISCARDED

HOT SODIUM HYDROXIDE (ALUMINA DISSOLVES IMPURITIES DO NOT)

$Al(OH)_3$ CRYSTALISED

ELECTROLYSIS AT 900°C

CRYOLITE $Na_3 AlF_6$ ALUMINA Al_2O_3

ANODE

CATHODE

FILTERED AND HEATED ($Al(OH)_3 \longrightarrow Al_2 O_3 + 3H_2O$)

MOLTEN ALUMINIUM

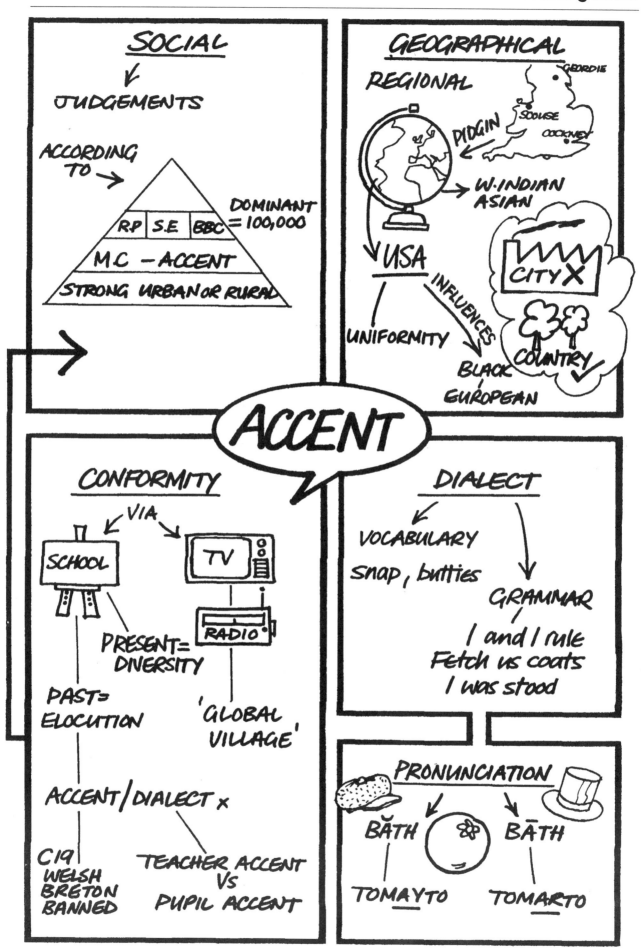

Making notes

❝ Read through your notes in the early evening so you can check up next day on anything you don't understand. ❞

❝ Make sure you will be able to read and understand your notes for revision. ❞

❝ Don't just read notes, test yourself. ❞

❝ When you're feeling a bit too tired to start on something new, making a fresh copy of a section of your notes is very satisfying. ❞

Revising from notes

There are a number of different ways of revising from notes:

1 **Reading notes just before the exam.** If you leave it this late, the sheer bulk of your notes will be daunting. As a result you will feel under stress even before you have begun to revise.

2 **Regular re-reading of notes** one day, one week, one month, three months and then six months after writing them. The Study Year Planner will help you to organise this. Although this may seem like a lot of work, in fact, it is particularly efficient because your learning is reinforced regularly.

3 **Underlining** key points in red, or with a highlighter pen.

4 **Making a pattern note** to summarise a whole section of notes.

5 **Re-drafting notes in a concise form**. You should write up your notes in best as soon as possible, ideally on the same day. Holidays are an excellent time to rewrite and condense your notes. Record (index) cards (126 x 79mm/5" x 3") are a handy format for this: they are pocket size and you can make use of the odd moment, in the bus queue for example, to revise.

FACT SHEET   Filing notes

It is frustrating and time wasting to have made notes on a subject and then not to be able to find them when you need them. Once you have made your notes you need to keep them in a place that is accessible, and in an order that's easy to follow. The same principle applies to your notes stored on computers, they must be clearly named and carefully stored (See page 131-2)

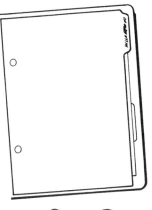

Making notes on file paper, rather than in a book, allows you to add and organize the material.

An **A4 Ring Binder** keeps your current notes together and is easy to carry about.

Dividers organise your file. You can buy them or make them yourself.

You don't have to carry all your notes around - you can keep your immediate notes and handouts on a **clipboard**, and file the others away.

Filing is part of the process of revision because
• you know where your notes are when you need them
• deciding where to file your notes means you have to look at them, and think about what category they belong to. This is a stimulus to your memory.

FACT SHEET   Storing notes 1

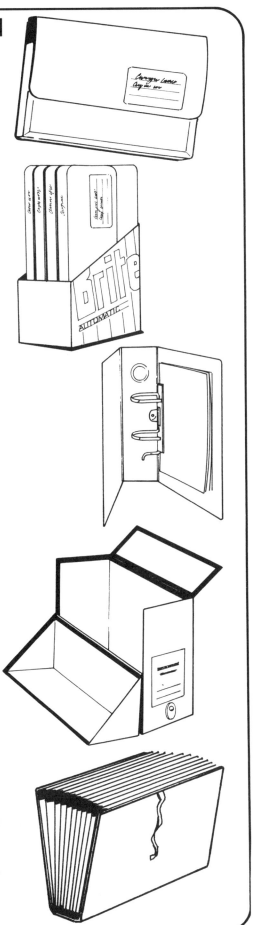

If you have a lot of notes then it is expensive to have to buy more ring binders. Instead you can file the notes which you are not currently using. There are a number of possibilities:

Large envelopes are convenient, or you can buy document wallets - it is better to buy the slightly more expensive ones which are glued at the sides so that your notes don't fall out. Clear plastic wallets are particularly useful because you can see immediately what is inside.

A large (E10) **washing powder box** can be cut to file these wallets of notes.

Lever arch files are a little more expensive than ring binders but can hold 2 or 3 times as many pages. They are not as easy to flick through as the ring binder.

Box files are hard wearing, but, without dividers, notes can be hard to find in them.

Concertina files hold more than the above, and are available in cardboard and metal versions. They allow you to see at a glance where your notes on a topic are. When full they are heavy to move.

FACT SHEET   Storing notes 2

Record cards are especially useful when you come to revising because they help you to concentrate on the essentials. You can put the chief points about a topic down, almost as if this was a plan for an exam essay. You can then carry the card round in your bag or pocket to revise in odd moments.

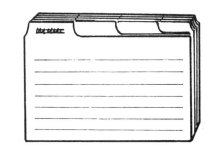

Record cards are available in three sizes: 127 x 76mm (5" x 3"), 152 x 101mm (6" x 4") and 203 x125 mm (8" x 5"). Any card that you are going to use a lot can be covered in clear adhesive plastic. You can file the cards in an old shoe box, with the help of a few dividers. Alternatively you can buy plastic boxes to file them in.

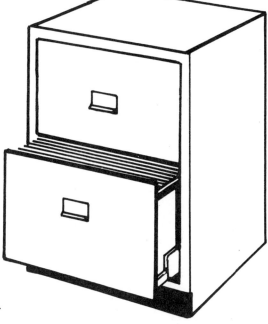

If you have a great number of notes, a small filing cabinet can be useful. It is possible to buy second-hand cabinets from some office equipment shops.

Arranging notes

It is best to arrange your notes thematically according to subject. Don't be afraid to rearrange them. and sub-divide as themes become clearer during your course of study.

If you have taken notes from several books and articles on a topic, you could arrange these notes alphabetically according to title or author. If you have been given a booklist, you could note on it where you have filed your notes.

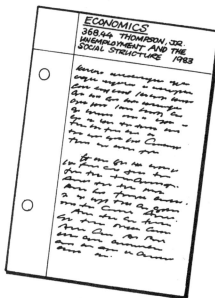

When taking notes from library books don't forget to note the code number, author and title, so you can quickly find the book again if you need it.

11 Abbreviations

Clear and accurate abbreviations are used widely to save time and space when writing notes. In some books and articles the words or phrases which are used frequently are written out at the beginning of the article and then abbreviated afterwards.

Some students write notes with connecting words missing:

Save time + space, be careful when reading notes, interpret accurately.

Another method of abbreviating notes is to leave out the vowels:

y cn stll rd ths bt y may nd sm vwls

Match the abbreviations in the boxes below with their corresponding words in the list.

```
∴   %   pp   NB   cf   op cit
ibid   et al   @   ∴   ie   ♀
min   h   c1475   C19   ♂   "
```

```
m   kg   s   V   °C   Cal   °F
l   Ar   Mr   ρ   log   ≥
>   ln   <   λ   J
```

General abbreviations

female ....

minutes ....

pages ....

therefore ....

about (date) ....

per cent ....

male ....

hours ....

compare ....

at   ....

because ....

in other words ....

century ....

in the work cited ....

and others ....

in the same place ....

note well ....

same as above, ditto ....

Scientific abbreviations

less than ....

litre ....

density ....

metre ....

logarithm ....

calorie ....

volt ....

degrees Fahrenheit ....

kilogram ....

wavelength ....

relative atomic mass ....

greater than ....

natural logarithm ....

degrees centigrade ....

relative molecular mass ....

greater than or equal to ....

second ....

joule ....

Note any other abbreviations of your own that you are going to use in your work.
You may also like to look for the Oxford Dictionary of Abbreviations in your library.

12 Library and research skills

SIDELINES & NOTES

Choosing a library

A good library will provide you with

- Up-to-date books, periodicals, newspapers, cassettes, CDs, videos and other resources on your subject
- Computer catalogue to allow easy and efficient access to information
- Computer facilities for word-processing and access to CD-Roms
- Access to the Internet, which may include electronic mail facilities, on-line services and electronic journals
- Expert advice on how to make the most of the library's facilities
- Photocopying facilities
- A quiet and convenient place to work, with an atmosphere that encourages supported self-study

Compare bookstocks and study facilities at the libraries nearest you.

It is a sensible idea at the beginning of your course to find out which libraries you can use within a reasonable travelling distance.

Other facilities which might be relevant to you include: picture loans, talks from visiting authors, details of courses and leisure activities.

Your library

The library at your place of study will automatically allow you to
- Borrow books
- Study in the library

However, the smaller the educational institution the more limited its library services will be in terms of
- Computer and photocopying facilities
- An up-to-date and extensive bookstock
- A wide range of reference sources
- Professional advice. Small libraries may be staffed by clerical assistants rather than by professional librarians

Library and research skills

In the UK 58% of the population are members of a library.

❛ *Ask how the system works because it's difficult at first.* ❜

❛ *Ask the staff. They get paid to help you.* ❜

HEADPHONES are avaailable if you wish to listen to cassettes.

Newspapers are located in the Reference Section

The public library

A local branch library may be useful for light reading, and for studying if it has a separate reference section. For serious study and research, however, you will need to go to the central library which will provide separate lending and reference libraries, as well as the sort of studious atmosphere which is an aid to self discipline and concentration.

If you are studying away from home you will be able to be a member of both your home public library and the public library at your place of study. Similarly, if you are not a full time student but work outside the local authority area in which you live then you will be able to join the library service of both authorities.

When you are applying for membership of a public library, take along with you some proof of your identity and address.

A local academic library

It may well be possible to use the library of a local college or university, for study and reference if you ask permission. These libraries will not, however, allow you to borrow books.

Getting to know your way round

By getting to know the library you intend to use most, you will
• Feel more at home there
• Know where to find the books you use most
• Be able to settle quickly to your work

Advice

At both large public libraries and college libraries you will be able to obtain expert advice. Look for 'Information' or 'Readers' Adviser' signs, or ask the assistants on the counter to direct you to the professional staff. One of the librarians may have a qualification in your subject.

Guides

Many libraries have some form of printed guide which lists their facilities and services. Some college libraries arrange special introductory sessions and tours or videos for new students.

Library plan

If there is a library plan on display this may reveal less obvious facilities of the library, eg a local studies collection, a slide library, a software library or information files generated in-house.

Browsing

This is an excellent way of getting to know the library, and also makes a break from your studies.

Finding a resource

Most libraries have replaced the traditional card catalogue with a far more versatile and user-friendly computer catalogue. The principle of using the Dewey decimal numbering system to classify resources remains the same (see Factsheet page 64). Each subject is given a code or classification number which is put on the spine of the book. Books are arranged by this number on the shelf.

How to find resources on a subject

Most libraries have enhanced the computer search facility by allocating a number of keywords to each resource. A subject or keyword search is the most effective route to access information on a particular subject. If there is nothing on your subject it might be listed under a different name. Try thinking of another word, perhaps a more general or more specific term. On the left below, for example, are some headings you might think of, and on the right are terms that they might be listed under in a keyword listing

> Adolescents   see Young People
> Andalucia   see Spain
> Argon   see Rare Gases

' Use the same library and try to get to know it. '

' Research makes you discover things for yourself, and that's one of the best ways of learning. '

Books on some subjects may be classified under a number of different headings according to the aspect and approach to the topic, for example

Computers:

Accountancy	657
Education	370.778
Graphic Arts	760
Management	658.05
Office Equipment	651.8
Programming	001.642
Social Effects	303.483

The suitability of any particular resource can sometimes be judged by the title but a more precise assessment can be made by highlighting the resource and asking for further details. The full keyword listing will reflect the subject content of the resource more accurately, while bibliographic details will indicate the relevance of a resource with regard to date, type and place of publication. Many libraries will have a printout facility so that you can retain a hard copy. You may be grateful for this when it comes to writing a bibliography at the end of your assignment.

How to find a resource if you know the author

An author search using the author's surname will give a listing of all the relevant resources held by the library and, where appropriate, by satellite libraries. This search route is often used to find fiction books. Students, having enjoyed reading a particular author, may wish to discover what other titles are available.

How to find a resource if you know the title

A title search is of limited use when researching a particular subject because title words frequently misrepresent or inadequately describe the content of the resource. As significant keywords will not necessarily appear in the title, a subject or keyword search is a much more thorough way of accessing information.

If a title search is required remember to ignore "The" and "A" at the beginning of the title.

The versatility of a computer catalogue permits searches using other fields such as Dewey code, publisher, ISBN (International Standard Book Number) or date of publication or media (eg book, video, CD Rom).

If the library has a book but you can't find it

If another reader has it then you can reserve the book for a small fee, but this might mean waiting several weeks - so plan well ahead. The catalogue will usually tell you if the book is on loan or is shelved elsewhere. Some libraries will allow you to reserve the book through the computer catalogue.

If the library doesn't have the book you want

You can ask the librarian to obtain it for you. Fill in a card giving as many details about the book as you can (author, title, date of publication, where you saw the book reviewed or mentioned). The librarian will decide to either purchase the book or borrow it through the Inter Library Loan System/British Library. In either case it may take quite a few weeks to come (though copies of journal articles can come within two or three days). You should tell the librarian if you have a deadline for using the book - it may not be possible to obtain the book as quickly as you need it. You can also arrange to borrow periodical articles.

Remember the resources you need may be in demand so plan well ahead.

Journals

In addition to books, a good academic library will subscribe to a large number of journals: Journals are used by academics to write papers about their research and ideas and therefore often contain the most up to date information on topics. Papers that are published in journals always have a summary or abstract at the beginning so it is quite easy to find out whether it is of any relevance to your subject. Try browsing in the journal section of your library. Look at the contents pages and turn to any papers that seem to be interesting. Read the abstract and if you find that interesting, go on to read the paper. Journal papers are not usually listed individually in the main library databases so browsing is the only way you will find out what is there.

Some computer databases (e.g. BIDS*) have what is known as a citation index. If you find a book or journal article that is relevant to your subject, you are easily able to find a number of other references by looking at its bibliography. However, this will only give you references to things written earlier. A citation index will let you find out whether that particular author has been included in the bibliographies of books and papers published later. This can provide a valuable list of more recent publications that are concerned with your particular subject.

SIDELINES & NOTES

*Bath Information and Data Services – http://www.bids.ac.uk access to BIDS is restricted to Higher Education institutions. Students in Higher Education will be given the passwords.

FACT SHEET

Library classification: the Dewey system

000	GENERAL WORKS
010	Bibliography
020	Librarianship
030	Encyclopedias
070	Journalism

100	PHILOSOPHY
110	Metaphysics
120	Epistemology
130	The paranormal
140	Specific philosophies
150	Psychology
160	Logic
170	Ethics
180	Ancient, medieval & Oriental philosophy
190	Modern western philosophy

200	RELIGION
210	Natural religion
220	The Bible
230	Christian theology
240	Moral theology
250	The local church; religious orders
260	Social theology
270	Church history
280	Christian churches & sects
290	Other religions

300	SOCIAL SCIENCES
310	Statistics
320	Political science
330	Economics
340	Law
350	Public administration
360	Social problems & services
370	Education
380	Commerce
390	Customs, folklore

400	LANGUAGE
410	Linguistics
420	English
430	German
440	French
450	Italian
460	Spanish; Portuguese
470	Latin
480	Clasical Greek
490	Other languages

500	PURE SCIENCES
510	Mathematics
520	Astronomy
530	Physics
540	Chemistry
550	Geology
560	Fossils
570	Anthropology; Biology
580	Botany
590	Zoology

600	TECHNOLOGY
610	Medicine
620	Engineering
630	Agriculture
640	Home economics, housecraft
650	Business & management
660	Chemical technology
670	Manufactures
680	Manufactures for specific purposes
690	Buildings

700	THE ARTS
710	Town & country planning
720	Architecture
730	Sculpture
740	Drawing
750	Painting
760	Graphic arts; prints
770	Photography
780	Music
790	Recreations; theatre & television; sport

800	LITERATURE
810	American
820	English
830	German
840	French
850	Italian
860	Spanish; Portuguese
870	Latin
880	Greek
890	Other literatures

900	GEOGRAPHY & HISTORY
910	Geography; travel
920	Biography
930	Ancient history
940	European history
950	Asian history
960	African history
970	North American history
980	South American history
990	History of other areas

13 Key reference resources

*If the information you need **must** be up-to-date, then check when the reference book was published.*

'*Reference books can be a great timesaver. Get to know the ones for your subject.*'

Some of these resources will be found in all libraries. Larger libraries should have them all in the latest edition. Many reference books are also available in electronic form, sometimes with update links via the internet.

Points to bear in mind when deciding which reference resources are most appropriate for your use:
- availability
- up-to-dateness
- ease and speed of use

Ask your librarian about your particular needs.

As you read through this section, note in the sidelines any resources which will be of particular interest to you. Later, check where they can be found in the library.

Dictionaries

There are a large number of useful one volume dictionaries, and new editions appear quite regularly. It would be a wise investment to buy a dictionary, such as *The Concise Oxford Dictionary*, for home use. The CD Rom version of this dictionary has sound to help pronunciation.

Oxford English Dictionary (OED)

This 20 volume dictionary is for scholarly, not everyday, use. It provides an historical record of the development and change of meaning of almost half a million words and phrases, and the definitions are illustrated by over two million quotations selected from general, literary, technical and other sources. As with many reference books, this resource is more versatile and user-friendly, though not necessarily quicker to use, in the CD-Rom format.

'*Keep a dictionary handy.*'

Roget's Thesaurus

This is probably more useful than a dictionary when you are writing an essay. If you are at a loss for the exact word or phrase, look up any equivalent you can think of in the index. This will then offer you a variety of shades of meaning. Choose the one closest to your requirements, and look up the number beside it in the main text of the thesaurus. Here you will find a keyword and sub-headings, followed by numerous synonyms.

Key reference resources

CD ROM encyclopedias are speedy and accessible, though multimedia images on some can mask a paucity of actual information.

Unfortunately some students have been unable to resist the temptation of downloading information from a CD ROM encyclopedia and then passing it off as their own work (for a comic example see the sidelines on page 132). Beware – this is obviously wrong, it's the opposite of learning and it will almost certainly be detected by your teacher or examiner.

Encyclopedias

Encyclopedia Britannica (USA) (CD ROM & book)
The CD Rom version allows for speedy searching by key word and for you to receive updated information via the internet. This is certainly the most comprehensive encyclopedia on CD Rom. Updated annually.

Grolier Encyclopedia (USA) (CD ROM)
Speedier and more fun than the Britannica. This doesn't have the scholarly depth of the above, but does offer a very lively, multimedia approach which is excellent for quick reference, an introduction to a topic. It has almost twice as many articles as Encarta, and also has more video and internet links. Updated annually. Mac & PC.

Microsoft Encarta Encyclopedia (CD ROM)
Highly visual encyclopedia which is widely available. PC only.

McGraw-Hill Encyclopedia of Science and Technology
20 scholarly volumes. Also on CD ROM.

World Book Encyclopedia
The best encyclopedia for school use. 22 volumes and on CD ROM.

Year books & annual publications

Britain: an official handbook
A single volume giving facts and figures on the economy, background material on overseas relations, information on Britain's cultural and sporting pursuits, and much more.

Guinness Book of Records
This popular annual is divided into subject sections with the information arranged thematically within each section.

Kelly's
This gives information on almost 100,000 different UK companies. There is a product index, products & services section.

Key Organisations
Carel Press' annual list of addresses of key organisations with e-mail and web sites. Includes a thematic guide, as well as sections on national, international and virtual museums, key libraries, tourist boards and universities.

Whitaker's Almanack
This guide to British and world affairs contains a great deal of miscellaneous information.

Who's Who
Over 30,000 biographies of people of influence and interest in all fields. Information, supplied by the people themselves, is given in a standard format of name, present position, date of birth, family details, education, career, publications, recreations and address.

Statistics

Annual Abstract of Statistics

Covers all aspects of UK economic, social and industrial life. Often gives comparative figures over a decade. (Office for National Statistics)

Fact File

A photocopiable, user-friendly, annual resource giving UK, European and international information and statistics on a very wide range of subjects from advertising to women. The raw data is also available on disc, allowing users to create their own charts. (Carel Press)

Social Trends

Detailed statistical charts, tables and commentary on the UK under headings such as 'Education' , 'Employment', and 'Lifestyles & Environment'. Statistics drawn from a wide range of government departments and other organisations. Annual. (Office for National Statistics)

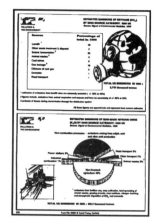

A page from Fact File

Further education & careers

British Qualifications

A guide to educational, technical, professional and academic qualifications. Also gives information on where to study different subjects. Published by the Careers & Occupational Information Centre (COIC).

Cassell Careers Encyclopedia

An independent, authoritative and comprehensive guide to careers, training and employment trends in Britain.

CVs and Applications

This helps you to present yourself on paper. It gives examples of CV layouts, application forms and letters, with tips on how to make your application eye-catching and informative. (Lifetime Careers)

Occupations

An annual reference book on careers and jobs. (COIC)

Official UCAS Guide

An annual publication of universities and colleges, their courses and entry requirements.

Sponsorship for Students

This covers the financial implications of further study and tells you all you need to know about sponsorship and being sponsored. (Hobson)

Which Degree

An annual, multi-volume guide to all full-time and sandwich first degree courses. Published by CRAC.

Key reference resources

Current issues and events

Essential Articles, *The resource file for issues*

A series of biennial volumes of thematically arranged journalism covering 157 issues and controversies from adoption to zoos. The articles are taken from over 220 different UK newspapers and magazines. (Carel Press)

Keesing's Record of World Events

This is a record of national and international current events with continually updated indexes. The information has been taken from the press and broadcasting.

The world

Europa World Yearbook

An annual reference guide to international organisations and to over 200 countries and territories.

Philip's World Handbook

An authoritative geographical reference work giving world maps, a gazetteer and statistics in a single volume.

Statesman's Year Book

A volume of international facts, figures and statistics. Countries are listed alphabetically, and information is arranged under headings such as 'Economy', 'Communications' and 'Energy & Natural Resources'. International organisations are also treated.

Times Atlas of the World

A standard reference work.

World Guide

'An alternative reference to the countries of our planet.' Biennial guide to 217 countries as seen from a Third World viewpoint. Particularly strong on global issues such as education and environment. (New Internationalist/ Instituto Del Tercer Mundo)

General & other works

Directory of Grant-Making Trusts

Biennial. (CAF Publications). Lists sources of funding available to the voluntary sector, and to some individuals.

Granger's Index to Poetry (USA)

Indexes according to title, first line, last line, author and subject. The latest edition indexes 79,000 poems in 400 anthologies.

Guinness Book of Knowledge

An authoritative compendium of knowledge with facts and diagrams on topics from The Calendar to Anthropology. There is a section on countries and counties of the UK.

New Grove Dictionary of Music & Musicians

20 volumes. The latest edition seeks to discuss everything related to music in history and in present-day musical life.

Oxford Dictionary of Quotations

This gives more than 17,000 quotations from 2,500 people arranged according to author. There is a useful keyword index.

Teenager's Guide to the Law

A reference guide dealing with the main areas of law affecting young people. Describes the legal rights of young people and lists useful contacts for further information and help. (Cavendish Publishing)

Writer's Handbook

Annual guide for writers and those involved in the media. Details publishers, national and regional newspapers, magazines, TV companies, picture libraries etc. (Macmillan)

Bibliographies & indexes

British Books in Print

Updated monthly on fiche and CD ROM. Includes all reported titles for the given month, and forthcoming publications. In one alphabetical sequence of authors, titles, inverted titles and references.

British Humanities Index (BHI)

Subject index to periodicals in the humanities. Quarterly with an annual cumulation. Available on CD ROM.

British National Bibliography (BNB)

Lists British publications by author and title. Published weekly, monthly, quarterly and annually. There are separate special editions on CD ROM for both schools and colleges.

Abstracts in New Technology and Engineering

Bi-monthly and annual index of articles in periodicals in technology arranged by subjects with an author index. Available on CD ROM.

14 Book skills

Selecting and rejecting

Reading lists

You may be given long and daunting reading lists. Some lists will helpfully note which books are

    ** essential

     * recommended

       background reading, or reference only

If your list isn't divided up like this, and you feel rather overwhelmed, then ask your teacher or lecturer for advice.

In the library

The essential skill, once you have located the relevant section in the library, is to reject unhelpful books as speedily as possible, thus leaving more time for using your chosen books.

Purpose: If you are clear about why you are looking at these books then your searching is much more likely to be successful. Are you looking for

• a specific piece of information?

• a general summary or introduction to a subject?

• a chart or illustration?

• the explanation of a difficult term?

• a variety of viewpoints on a controversial subject?

• a thorough and scholarly treatment of a subject?

• references to further reading?

If you are going to make notes from a book note down the author, title, library code number, date of publication and page references. You never know when you may need to refer to the book again.

If the book is a library book then do not mark it in any way.

Just because a book is in the library, it does not mean that it is either useful or well written. Don't waste a lot of time trying to read books that you find difficult to understand because the sentences are too long or there is too much jargon. Look around and you are likely to find another book that is well written.

You can use the checklist on the next two pages to help you.

Assessing a book: a checklist

Title

Remember that a short title can rarely indicate the scope of a book.

Subtitle

This may indicate a level of difficulty, e.g. 'a student's guide'

Author

How qualified and experienced is the author in this field? Look for information about the author at the front of the book or on the cover. If the author has published any other works these may also be listed.

Publisher

A particular publisher may have a good reputation in a certain area, or simply be known as a reputable publisher.

Blurb

This is the information given on a book's back cover, or on the inside flap of a hardback's jacket. It is usually written by the publisher to sell the book, and often claims more for a book than an author would. Still it is a useful brief guide to what the book hopes to cover and achieve. It is sometimes more a statement of intent than of fact.

Date of publication

This appears on the reverse of the title page. The first © copyright sign, and the author's name, is the date of original publication, but remember that many books will have been written several months before this date. A new **impression**

First published 1998
Fourth impression 2000

means the book has sold out, and been reprinted, usually with minor corrections. This information may be presented as follows in more modern books:

     Printing number 1 2 3 4 5 6 7 8 9 10

with successive numbers being deleted at each reprint.

A new **edition** means that the author has thoroughly revised the text, and perhaps added new sections, while rewriting others, and bringing the whole work up to date.

First published 1997
Reprinted 1997, 1998
Second edition 1999

Place of publication

This can be important in some subjects. If the book was published abroad the publisher's address will show this. If the book is simply an English translation, or an English edition of a book originally published overseas, then this will be stated:

First published in the United States 1997
First published in England 1998

Contents

This reveals at a glance the framework of the book. Do not feel that you have to read a book from beginning to end. This is only really important with novels. From the contents, decide which chapters may be of value. Read the first and last paragraphs of these chapters - this should give you some idea as to whether they contain information that will be of value to you (see chapter 15).

List of illustrations/diagrams

Older books often have a list of illustrations. A list of diagrams can indicate how comprehensive, and up to date, a book's coverage is. Turning first to a diagram or table may save you a considerable amount of reading.

Preface

This may state who the book is written for.

Introduction or preface

This is written after the rest of the book, and often summarises the author's thinking about the subject as well as stating who the book is written for.

Conclusion

If the book has a conclusion, reading it first can save you a lot of time. If you then decide to read the book through you will have a clear sense of the author's direction right from the beginning. Alternatively the opening or closing paragraphs of chapters may act as summaries.

Index

Some books have a separate name and subject index. Illustrations are referred to in **bold type** or *italic* and in many books major references to a topic, rather than just passing references, are noted in bold type.

Trade Councils 17, 43, **61-66**
Trades Unions 16,19, 31, 31, **48-60**
Unemployment 9,12,17, 33-36
Unions *see* Trades Unions
Wages 4,18, 27, *38*, 50-51

The term you are looking up may not be the term used in the index. Think of synonyms and other possible entries. If the book is American it is particularly likely that a different term will have been used.

Bibliography (or References)

This is the list of sources which the writer has consulted. It will quickly indicate how broad and thorough the writer's research has been. By checking the dates of publication for the books listed in the bibliography you will be able to judge how current the author's work is.

Abbreviations used in footnotes in books

ibid. = in the same book as noted in the last footnote
pp. = pages
op. cit. = in the book already mentioned
cf. = compare
ff. = and the following pages
passim = to be found throughout a particular book

15 Reading

SIDELINES & NOTES

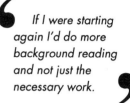

If I were starting again I'd do more background reading and not just the necessary work.

Reading for study

The largest part of a student's study time is spent reading. It is important that you learn to

- manage the quantity of necessary reading effectively
- read quickly with understanding
- avoid irrelevant reading
- identify different styles of reading which will be effective for various reading purposes
- gain access to the most useful material available
- read actively and resist episodes of passive reading which can arise
- develop a questioning attitude to written material

Throughout this chapter we will consider these points and return to them to analyse the effectiveness of your reading.

Now complete the first two columns of the table on the next page. Write in brief details of all the reading you have done in the last week or so. Consider all reading: texts, questions, essays, novels, lecture notes, articles, newspapers, computer printouts and screens.

Reading table

As you work through this chapter, complete this table

Reading matter	1 Time taken (mins)	2 Reading strategy	3 Skimming	4 Most effective strategy	5 Vocabulary	6 Usefulness	7 SQ3R

Reading strategies

You always have a purpose when you read. Reading a novel for enjoyment is different from reading the same novel for appreciation on a literature course. In the same way, if you are looking for a piece of information then it is not necessary to read a book from page one to the end as you would read a novel.

This table describes six different reading strategies.

Reading strategy	Description	Purpose
Detailed reading	Reading the whole passage carefully and thoughtfully trying to appreciate every point the author is making.	Complete understanding
Skimming	Finding out what a chapter or book is about.	General impression
Critical reading	Some authors write to persuade. You need to separate fact from opinion.	Making up your mind
Analytical reading	Looking at the mechanics of the writing, studying the writer's skill.	Appreciate style and structure
Reading for **enjoyment**	Reading at whatever pace suits you. The more you read, the better reader you become.	Pleasure
Scanning (Reading for Information)	Looking for a specific detail by running your eye over the page.	Fact finding

Enter in the reading table (page 74) which reading strategy you think you used in your recent reading.

Skimming

You will be more effective, and have more time, if skimming is part of your reading routine. Skimming can be used in two ways:
- in the selection and rejection of chapters or books for reading.
- as preparation before reading a chapter or book.

The volume of reading most students face is enormous: text books, set books, recommended book lists, periodicals, reports, and much special subject reading as well.

> *Reading a book is like rewriting it for yourself.*
>
> Angela Carter, author

> *There are different techniques of reading for different types of books. If you're looking for a certain bit of information then don't read the whole page.*

Reading

Skimming allows you to sort the wheat from the chaff and creates the time for you to concentrate on important sections of reading matter. When you skim you do not read every word, instead you read:

- the title and subheadings
- the first sentence from each paragraph (or the first paragraph of a chapter)
- the last sentence of a passage (or the last paragraph of a chapter)
- a summary of the chapter, if there is one
- pay attention to any diagrams, charts or graphs.

Try skimming the passage *Is the Ocean Bottom Moving?* on the next page. Some questions are set at the bottom of this page, read these first: these are your reading purpose. Before you start, re-read the set of bullet points above.

Questions

1 What is the passage about?

. . . .

. . . .

2 Does the passage explain why the ocean floor has few older rocks?

. . . .

. . . .

Is the Ocean Bottom Moving?

The ocean bottom is very interesting to oceanographers from many points of view. For one thing they find that the sedimentary rocks that exist on the ocean bottom are much younger than any similar rocks they find on the continents. In fact, no deposits on the ocean floor seem to be older than a couple of hundred million years, whereas many rocks on the continents are far older than this. For many years geologists have been asking, "Why aren't there older rocks on the ocean bottom?" and "Where do the older rocks go?"

Furthermore, the mud layers covering the rocks on the bottom of the ocean - the sediments - are continually being deposited, and yet the thickness of this overall layer remains very thin. Again, scientists ask: "Where do these sediments go?" "Why aren't the sediments much thicker on the ocean bottom than we find them to be?"

The answers to these questions have been found in modern measurements which indicate that the ocean bottom must be in motion. It is moving at a speed of about 1.5 to 15 centimetres a year, and it seems to be doing so in a manner that suggests that the continents also are moving. Apparently the continents can be thought of as floating in a "sea" of basalt (that is, the ocean bottom rocks).

Scientists think that many millions of years ago all the continents were joined together in two huge land masses, called Laurasia and Gondwanaland. Later on in geological time, Laurasia split into North America, Europe, and Asia, while South America, Africa, Antarctica, and Australia were formed from Gondwanaland. But the final picture is apparently not complete, for the sea bottom is still moving and evidently the continents are moving too. Where they will be a few million years from now, scientists can only guess.

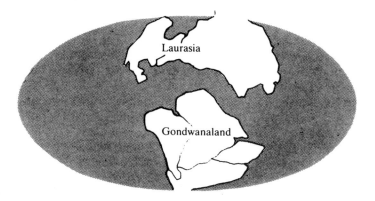

The two primeval continents, Laurasia, consisting of North America, Europe, and Asia; and Gondwanaland, consisting of South America, Africa, Antarctica, and Australia.

As far as oceanographers can now tell, the reason for this movement is that the rock beneath the earth's crust (the mantle) is a somewhat fluid substance. It will move in much the same manner as water, but of course much more slowly. With the earth being warmer in the interior, convective currents or vertical heat motions are set up in much the same way that air in a room moves from the floor to the ceiling when an electric heater is placed on the floor. Of course, when the moving mantle material reaches the underside of the crystal rocks (the ocean bottom), it spreads out to the sides. It is this horizontal motion that causes the ocean bottom and the continents to move.

Eventually, the mantle material must return to the interior of the earth, because any such material that comes from there must be replaced. In this manner, the older rocks on the underside of the oceanic crust are dragged down into the earth, which explains why the older rocks cannot be found. Similarly, the older sediments are also carried away as they build up. Measurements have been made that indicate that the rocks very close to the mid-Atlantic ridge in the North Atlantic Ocean have very recently risen from the interior of the earth, while at points farther away from the mid-Atlantic ridge, it was found that the age of the rocks increased. Thus, by noting the rock age measurements and the distance between samples, it is possible for scientists to calculate the rate at which the sea floor is spreading - which works out to be between 1.5 and 15 centimetres per year.

Extract from *Oceanography* Jerome Williams, Franklin Watts Ltd.

You can practise skimming while reading newspapers or magazines. Skimming is a very useful preparation for reading a chapter or book in detail. This enables you to appreciate the structure of the topic and how parts of it inter-relate. As you skim, your mental set is developing; your concentration will focus more strongly on your work rather than on any distractions.

Summaries

By reading the summary you will become aware of the destination of an argument or proof; this allows insight into the thinking which arises en route. Most of us read study books as we would read a thriller, the plot develops and comes to a conclusion. When reading study material it is essential that there is no mystery about what is to follow.

Indicate on the reading table (column 3) which parts of your reading were skimmed before you read them in detail. Use a ✔. Put a ✗ next to any part of your recent reading which would have been better skimmed, i.e. it would have helped your understanding and saved you time.

Reading matter	1 Time taken (mins)	2 Reading strategy	3 Skimming	4 Most effective strategy	5 Vocabulary	6 Usefulness	7 SQ3R
Industry text	3 hrs in all	Mainly detailed	✔	1 Skim 2 Detailed	✔	A	SQ3R
Sunday paper	30		✗			D	

Scanning

When you scan a page or a chapter you are looking for a piece of information. The brain can recognise what it is searching for extremely quickly, much faster than the time it takes to read the text.

Run your eye through *Come on get happy*. What was the 'flow' theory developed at the University of Chicago?

. . . .

. . . .

Try scanning again to discover 'an instant cure for mild depression'. (A pen might help to guide your eye when scanning. Obviously you don't continue to scan when you have located your information.)

. . . .

. . . .

Come on, get happy

So you think joy is out of your reach? Think again, says **Jerome Burne.**
It's there for the taking.

As a nation, we don't do too badly in the pleasure stakes. A European survey last month conducted by ARISE (Associates for Research into the Science of Enjoyment) found that we are second only to the Dutch in enjoying ourselves, although we tended to feel more guilty afterwards.

But Colin Roth's new book, *Being Happy* (Kingfield Press £9.95) could push us to the coveted number one slot. It's an eccentric read but then research shows that eccentrics are generally happier than the rest of us. Roth suggests that there are two sorts of people: those who see life in a traditional feminine way - the Clingers - and those who see it in a traditional masculine way - the Loners. If you are a female Clinger, life will be less problematic than if you are a male Clinger, and vice versa. The secret of happiness is to work out which you are.

Dividing people into types is an age-old idea and there is no evidence that Roth's division is more firmly-based than anyone else's. But we do know a lot about happiness. For instance, Professor Richard Davidson of Madison University has located it in the left pre-frontal lobe of the brain, ie just above the left eyebrow. People with lots of activity there are the Pollyannas. But the good news is that if your lobe is sluggish you can boost it by thinking positive thoughts, exercising, smiling and aiming for achievable goals.

But even without such concentrated effort there seems to be a happiness constant in society. A basic level of material possessions is necessary, but adding more doesn't seem to make much difference. Americans and most Europeans are, on average, twice as wealthy as they were 35 years ago, yet surveys show them to be no more happy. People are generally happier in a relationship than alone - fewer than 25 per cent of single Americans report being very happy as compared to 40 per cent of married people.

Feeling in control of your life or your job helps. Three out of five people who say they are in control say they are happy. Healthy people are happier than the sick but the disabled are about as happy as the rest of us. Even people paralysed in car accidents described themselves as happy three weeks later. This points to another fact about happiness: it is relative.

An instant cure for mild depression is something really awful happening - like bankruptcy or the death of your family. Compared to that, your current life - only a moment earlier a desert - suddenly seems like paradise. Take lottery wins: if you think you have won £10,000 but it turns out to be only £1,000, you feel cheated. But an unexpected £1,000 is a delightful surprise. When, after a year, big lottery-winners have got used to their new lifestyle, they say they are as happy as a paraplegic says he is.

But how can you set about getting happiness? Mihaly Csikszentmihalyi, professor of psychology and education at the University of Chicago has been trying to answer the question for 20 years. He believes the key to happiness is something he calls the "flow". This is the state you are in when you are doing something that completely absorbs you. It comes when you are pushed to the limit of your ability but not beyond it, when you are challenged, but you can handle it.

Csikszentmihalyi started by studying artists who became totally caught up in painting or composing, but soon realised that flow was wider than that. "People can get a feeling of flow from dangerous sports like mountain climbing or driving fast," he says. "But it can also come from painting or reading a good book. The point is that it is something people do for its own sake. They are not looking for any external reward."

To find out how flow fits into everyday life he recently fixed up some high-school children with an electronic paging device to find out how they felt about their activities through the day. They had to say how challenging it was for them and how skilled they were at it. Activities where both challenge and skill are high, such as singing or studying, are flow experiences. Fighting, however, is a high challenge low skill activity which produces anxiety.

But you could simply try "living mindfully" by appreciating that whatever is going on in your life - your awful job, unfaithful partner, weight problem - there are many moments every day that can bring happiness. Practise noticing those times in the day when you realise you are perfectly happy. It could be just a smell, a colour, the way the morning light falls on a table, a joke with a friend. The trick is to become aware, concentrate on those moments and not allow your chronic complaints to swamp everything.

Five steps to a happier you

1 Start to build a new picture of yourself. Make a list of your positive attributes - kind, generous, attentive. Then list your skills - play the piano, great cook. Then say them out loud to yourself.

2 Ask your most trusted friends for some positive statements about yourself.

3 Keep a journal and write down all those good things that happen to you and the positive things that people say to you.

4 Start to recognise your own interior critic who will put you down and belittle you. Begin to challenge those self-criticisms. On close examination, they usually turn out to be wild exaggerations. Rephrase them in a more positive light.

5 When you do feel low ask yourself how you can avoid becoming stuck in that feeling. Do you need to see someone, take exercise, do something different?

from *The Guardian*

Reading

Practise reading strategies

The exercise which follows is designed to give you practice in choosing and using the best reading strategy. There are three different passages each requiring a different reading strategy, or strategies, in order to answer some questions. The questions are given at the start of each passage. Read each question carefully as it will become your purpose for reading and will help you to decide which of the six reading strategies (outlined on page 75) will be most appropriate. When you have chosen, read the passage according to that style and then answer the questions.

These questions are for the passage opposite *Sleep more, drink less and learn better – dream on.*

Question: What is the main characteristic of REM sleep?

. . . .

. . . .

. . . .

Reading strategy used: [   ]

Question: What was the specific evidence which cast doubt on results from rats being applied to human sleep behaviour?

. . . .

. . . .

. . . .

Reading strategy used: [   ]

Question: Why do Smith's results on students lend support to theories of REM sleep being important for transfer of learning from short-term to long-term memory?

. . . .

. . . .

. . . .

Reading strategy used: [   ]

Sleep more, drink less and learn better – dream on!

Sleep is not simple. Last night you slept in 90 minute cycles and in each cycle your brain showed at least three different types of activity. Scientists have known about different types of sleep for many years; whilst they can agree on some of the ways sleep is important to us, they disagree on the details of the theories. For example most scientists agree that sleep is a form of hibernation providing an opportunity to rebuild our energy supplies for when we wake up. Some believe that sleep is a period of mental tidying-up when the brain decides what to keep of the previous days events and what to discard.

REM sleep seems to have some link to memory. REM sleep is characterised by Rapid Eye Movement and occurs at a time when the brain shows a frenzy of more rapid and random brain waves - almost like those that occur when we are awake. It is during REM sleep that we dream. Now there is an emerging school of thought that believes REM sleep is the time when memories are laid down. Rats and students who have been in intense learning situations, such as how to get out of a maze and cramming for exams respectively, have more REM when they sleep. More importantly depriving rats and students of REM, by waking them when REM starts, leads to weaker remembering of what they had learned. REM seems to be particularly important in humans for casting "know-how" rather than simple facts, into long term memory.

How does REM link with memory? During REM the main brain wave is known as the theta rhythm. In rats it is around 5 - 10 Hertz in the hippocampus which is the part of the brain which serves as a short term memory store. Research has shown that it is this theta rhythm which reshapes neuron connections.

The synapse is where the neurons join, there are millions of neurons and millions of synapses in the brain. When something enters the memory an electrical impulse crosses the synapse - a connection between neurons is made. When it is remembered the electrical impulse fires across the same synapse again. Some scientists believe that the synapses that fire at the peak of a theta wave become stronger and those that fire at the theta trough become weaker. In this way the hippocampus sorts out which of the memories of the previous day should be kept - and transferred to long-term memory in the cortex - and which should be lost.

The REM theta rhythm in the hippocampus of humans is not so prominent and the link with learning may not be as strong as it is for rats. If the theory which links REM to memory holds, it has major implications for students learning for exams - get lots of sleep and the more you dream the better!

For some students there is some bad news - scientists have shown that alcohol reduces the amount of REM sleep. Two pints of beer will cut REM sleep by half. Ironically this research also confirms the link with memory. Some students from Trent University, Ontario were taught a logic puzzle. It involved sequencing symbols using some rules. Half the students were given alcohol on the night of their learning, the others were not. The students who had taken alcohol performed 30% worse than those that had not. The researcher, Carlyle Smith, also administered his test to volunteers and recorded their performances a week later. When he considered the results he said " I can always pick out a group who have stayed up way beyond their bedtime and had a lot of alcohol. It's worse if they've done both."

M Coles

Reading

These questions are for the fiction passage opposite, *The common good*

Question: If you were in Jim's place would the shorthand writer in the courtroom have such a strong effect on you?

. . . .

. . . .

. . . .

Reading strategy used: [   ]

Question:
To what extent has the writer adopted the style of his character, Jim, in this extract?

. . . .

. . . .

. . . .

How effective is the flashback technique used here?

. . . .

. . . .

. . . .

Reading strategy used: [   ]

Question: Is this a fair description of the way police behave during marches and in court?

. . . .

. . . .

. . . .

Reading strategy used: [   ]

The common good

Jim got a real shock of surprise when Sergeant Webster took the stand. For a start he wasn't in uniform. He was about forty, and very smartly dressed in a neat grey suit and a snowy white shirt. He had dark curly hair and a sort of friendly, pleasant face. For a moment Jim couldn't believe it was the same bloke. He had a sudden, crazy, notion that they'd put someone else in the witness box, someone pretending to be the sergeant. But that was daft. Even his voice was different, though; soft, and calm, and reasonable.

'I swear by Almighty God that the evidence that I give shall be the truth, the whole truth and nothing but the truth.'

It was absurd. Jim shivered. He remembered the sergeant's snarling, contorted face as he'd grabbed his arm and twisted it up his back until he'd screamed. He remembered the way, later, in the police station, he'd punched him in the stomach, and kicked him, and spat in his face. It was unbelievable.

The Sergeant's evidence was brief, and to the point, and sounded utterly reasonable. On the day of the march, he said, he had been in command of a group of thirty constables out of the total force of several hundreds. The area in which he had been controlling the crowds had been a particularly violent one, and several policemen had been injured, some of them seriously. The crowd, which had consisted mostly of Asians, with pockets of politically motivated whites, had been abusive and highly provocative. At first insults, then stones, sticks and bottles had been thrown. He had led several charges into the crowd, and made several arrests. On one of the charges he had seen the defendant, James Arthur Barker, holding a half-wallbrick which he clearly intended to throw at the police. His right arm was drawn back, his body was in a throwing stance, and he was shouting obscenities at the advancing officers. Yes, he could identify James Arthur Barker as the youth in the court; there. He was arrested and taken to Albert Road police station where he was formally cautioned, and charged with threatening behaviour and carrying an offensive weapon. At the police station he had been abusive, violent and had attempted to punch two police officers and kick another in the groin. A certain amount of force had had to be applied to bring him under control.

The sergeant looked round the court with a pleasant, honest look when he'd said his piece. Jim looked at his solicitor, Mr Ellerman, half expecting him to jump up and tear the story to pieces. Then he remembered. Mr Ellerman had said he wasn't going to cross-examine unless something was said that they weren't going to break down in their own evidence. He knew what he was doing, Jim was sure of that. He tried to relax, but he was shaken. It was incredible. It was a pack of lies, it was awful. Mr Ellerman indicated that he had no questions and the sergeant smiled and stepped down. As Jim looked up, so did the shorthand girl, and their eyes met. He felt a deep blush rise in his cheeks. He felt ashamed. What must she be thinking of him? It was awful.

From *A sense of shame and other stories* Jan Needle, Andre Deutsch

Return to the reading table (page 74) and write in column 4 the reading strategy which would have been most effective for each piece of your reading.

Reading

"
I took a speed reading course, learning to read straight down the middle of the page, and I was able to go through 'War and Peace' in 20 minutes. It's about Russia.
"

Woody Allen

Reading Speed

It is a tempting thought that we might double our rate of learning if we could read twice as fast. A student reads to learn and learning is a process which takes time. If we read faster than we can learn, confusion, misconceptions and poor recall are likely to result.

It is useful to consider reading and learning as one. When the information is easy to understand, because it is familiar or is closely linked to existing knowledge, then it is more efficient to increase the speed of reading. Harder material demands a slower reading rate; perhaps reading it twice is likely to yield a better understanding. In other words good students will vary their reading speed to suit the reading matter.

Research suggests that students slow down when they read difficult material but that they are unlikely to speed up when straightforward text and ideas are studied.

A flexible approach to reading speed will develop only with practice. The first stage is to identify the appropriate reading strategy. Detailed reading will often be required but should not be the automatic choice. Newspapers contain such a variety of articles that you can practise all of the different reading strategies. Having identified the appropriate strategy try to consciously control the rate at which you read. Notice the difference in the speed at which you read.

Using a newspaper:

- **Skim** the first few pages to find which story you most want to read.

- **Read** the story carefully, be aware of your reading rate.

- **Scan** the classified advertisements for a particular object you might like to buy.

- **Read** the newspaper's opinion column (the editorial). Separate fact from opinion.

Reasons for poor reading

1   Failure to recognise your reading purpose. Without a clear idea of why you are reading you are unlikely to be effective.

2   Failure to vary the pace of reading: this results in too slow or too fast processing of the information in the brain. During a slow phase the reader is more easily distracted, during a fast phase the reader will become confused.

3   Slow readers will lose the sense of what they are reading more easily. They will recognise this has happened and back-track. This takes time and further delays the appreciation of the piece.

4   Readers who do not recognise the 'markers' in the text (headings, paragraphs, introduction, conclusion, graphs and charts, order in arguments) will find it difficult to make good sense of the passage.

5   Pronouncing the words as you read slows down reading. This habit, often stemming from the time when we were first taught to read, must be broken. The best way to do this is to read more quickly so that vocalisation is impossible; light reading matter should be used for these exercises.

6   Failure to make notes, underline key words or use other forms of active reading always reduces effectiveness.

7   A limited vocabulary is a serious hindrance to effective and efficient reading and understanding. (See **Widening your vocabulary** page 109)

Put a ✔ in column 5 of the reading table if the reading matter had no words which you needed to check for meaning.

Rate how useful the material in the reading table is from the viewpoint of your studies. Use a scale A (very useful) to E (useless). Enter this in column 6.

Learn and remember: SQ3R

SQ3R is a very well known method of reading and remembering. Good students, about to employ SQ3R, will have a clear idea of what they need to learn. The first task is to **S**kim the book or chapter to make sure it is relevant to your study. By skimming you will also prepare your mental set and you will be less likely to be distracted.

Skim

Of course skimming is a useful way of getting into your stride. You should then frame your study purpose as a **Q**uestion or questions. Bear these in mind as you read, because they are your reading purpose and they

Question

ensure active reading. It is very easy to read mechanically without thinking about the reading matter.

You must be alert, active and enquiring as you read.

Read

The next stage is to **R**ead the book or chapter carefully, paying attention to graphs, diagrams and charts. If it is your own book consider using a yellow highlighter pen to draw your attention to important points. Clarify any points and check the meaning of any words you don't understand, as soon as you can.

Review

Now you must **R**eview the material. Have you answered the questions you set yourself? If not, you need to reread the relevant section. This period of review allows your brain time to order the new information (see page 43-44). If the work is important it should be reviewed again after a day and then after a week and so on. After carrying out the first four stages you should **R**emember the work more clearly.

Remember

Practise SQ3R on the passage from *The drive for power*. Before you start, read the questions which will be your purpose for reading.

Question: What evidence is there to suggest that the men behind the Industrial Revolution were scientists and men of conscience rather than hard-headed businessmen?

After each stage of SQ3R complete the checklist below.

Skim:
What is *The drive for power* about?   ❏
Is it likely to answer the question?   ❏
Do you appreciate the structure of the passage?   ❏

Question:
Are you clear about what information you are seeking in the text?   ❏
Have any more questions arisen during the reading of the passage? ❏

Read:
Are there any words you need to look up?   ❏
What are the key words?   ❏

Review:
Would you be able to answer the question? Review the passage again
if you need to.   ❏

Remember:
Which revision method would you use to remember this material?   ❏

Complete the reading table (page 74) by writing SQ3R in column 7 for any part of your study reading which might be better done using this method.

From **The drive for power**

The men who made the Industrial Revolution are usually pictured as hardfaced businessmen with no other motive than self-interest. That is certainly wrong. For one thing, many of them were inventors who had come into business that way. And for another, a majority of them were not members of the Church of England but belonged to a puritan tradition in the unitarian and similar movements. John Wilkinson was much under the influence of his brother-in-law Joseph Priestley, later famous as a chemist, but who was a Unitarian minister and was probably the pioneer of the principle, 'the greatest happiness of the greatest number'.

Joseph Priestley, in turn, was scientific adviser to Josiah Wedgwood. Now Wedgwood we usually think of as a man who made marvellous tableware for aristocracy and royalty: and so he did, on rare occasions, when he got the commission. For example, in 1774 he made a service of nearly a thousand highly decorated pieces for Catherine the Great of Russia, which cost over £2000 - a great deal of money in the coin of that day. But the base of that tableware was his own pottery, creamware; and in fact all the thousand pieces, undecorated, cost less than £50, yet looked and handled like Catherine the Great's in every way except for the hand-painted idylls. The creamware which made Wedgwood famous and prosperous was not porcelain, but a white earthenware pottery for common use. That is what the man in the street could buy, at about a shilling a piece. And in time that is what transformed the kitchens of the working class in the Industrial Revolution.

Wedgwood was an extraordinary man: inventive, of course, in his own trade, and also in the scientific techniques that might make his trade more exact. He invented a way of measuring the high temperatures in the kiln by means of a sort of sliding scale of expansion in which a clay test-piece moved. Measuring high temperatures is an ancient and difficult problem in the manufacture of ceramics and metals, and it is fitting (as things went then) that Wedgwood was elected to the Royal Society.

Josiah Wedgwood was no exception; there were dozens of men like him. Indeed, he belonged to a group of about a dozen men, the Lunar Society of Birmingham (Birmingham was then still a scattered group of industrial villages), who gave themselves the name because they met near the full moon. This was so that people like Wedgwood, who came from a distance to Birmingham, should be able to travel safely over wretched roads that were dangerous on dark nights.

But Wedgwood was not the most important industrialist there: that was Matthew Boulton, who brought James Watt to Birmingham because there they could build the steam engine. Boulton was fond of talking about measurement; he said that nature had destined him to be an engineer by having him born in the year 1728, because that is the number of cubic inches in a cubic foot. Medicine was important in that group also, for there were new and important advances being made. Dr William Withering discovered the use of digitalis in Birmingham. One of the doctors who has remained famous, who belonged to the Lunar Society, was Erasmus Darwin, the grandfather of Charles Darwin. The other grandfather? Josiah Wedgwood.　　　　　⫸

Societies like the Lunar Society represent the sense of the makers of the Industrial Revolution (that very English sense) that they had a social responsibility. I call it an English sense, though in fact that is not quite fair; the Lunar Society was much influenced by Benjamin Franklin and by other Americans associated with it. What ran through it was a simple faith: the good life is more than material decency, but the good life must be based on material decency.

It took a hundred years before the ideals of the Lunar Society became reality in Victorian England. When it did come, the reality seemed commonplace, even comic, like a Victorian picture postcard. It is comic to think that cotton underwear and soap could work a transformation in the lives of the poor. Yet these simple things - coal in an iron range, glass in the windows, a choice of food - were a wonderful rise in the standard of life and health. By our standards, the industrial towns were slums, but to the people who had come from a cottage, a house in a terrace was a liberation from hunger, from dirt, and from disease; it offered a new wealth of choice. The bedroom with the text on the wall seems funny and pathetic to us, but for the working class wife it was the first experience of private decency. Probably the iron bedstead saved more women from childbed fever than the doctor's black bag, which was itself a medical innovation.

These benefits came from mass production in factories. And the factory system was ghastly; the schoolbooks are right about that. But it was ghastly in the old traditional way. Mines and workshops had been dank, crowded and tyrannical long before the Industrial Revolution. The factories simply carried on as village industry had always done, with a heartless contempt for those who worked in them.

From *The Ascent of Man*, Jacob Bronowski, BBC and Angus & Robertson

FACT SHEET   The best conditions for reading

It is easy to underestimate the importance of the correct level of lighting and comfort for a reader. Highly motivated readers will read standing on a train, in front of a television set or in a busy canteen or refectory. Nevertheless when the motivation is lower, reading conditions become more important.

Make sure the text is evenly lit. A very bright light can produce too sharp a contrast between print and the background. Eye fatigue can cause headaches which can cut short study sessions. Some study lamps with 60 or 100 watt bulbs can create this effect. Use a low power lamp, or diffuse or reflect the light from a high power lamp. Trying to read in poor light also strains the eyes. Poor lighting is quickly identified but sometimes, . when a study session continues into the evening, the lighting conditions deteriorate slowly enough to deceive.

A good posture when reading is important. So much time is spent reading that the effect of poor posture can remain with us days, weeks or even years later. You should try to keep your back straight, sit in an upright chair with your back against the back of the chair. The reading material should be at a height which makes it possible for you to keep your neck and shoulders from bending forward too much. Desks and study surfaces are constructed with this in mind and if it proves difficult for you to read in this way, your eyesight might need attention. It is helpful to vary your reading position and location from time to time. This movement is healthy and can improve your concentration.

16 Writing

Many courses are now modular. Students need to meet strict deadlines throughout the course. This requires an organised approach to study, particularly when an assignment is set. Whether or not your course is modular, careful planning will enable you to stagger the workload.

What will you be asked to write?

At school up to the age of 16, most of your writing told a story in one way or another.

Creative writing asks for an imaginative response usually written in story form.

Factual assignments ask you to "describe", "give an account of" or "narrate" (tell the story of) something. Facts are usually more important than opinions in this type of assignment, and you rarely have the chance to give your own viewpoint or interpretation. Instead you need to show that you know the answers to questions about your subject such as

What happened?
How did it happen?
When?
Where?

In **scientific** assignments you have to explain, for example, a theory, process or investigation.

In post-16 education, most tasks are **analytical**. This requires you to interpret and comment on one aspect of a subject, for example

- Discuss the effects of public health reform on social conditions in Victorian England.
- How significant a role does fate play in the novels of Thomas Hardy?

> " At college there are more long assignments, they involve more thought and you can't just rely on the teacher's notes. "

- Was the dissolution of the monasteries primarily a religious, economic or political phenomenon?

Read the following list of essay titles and note in the sidelines beside each whether a factual or analytical essay is required:

- "I object to the National Lottery because it encourages gambling and because it takes money from those who are least able to afford it, but who are desperate to escape their situation...I am not impressed by the argument that it raises money for good causes. If we think things are worth supporting then we should be prepared to pay for them out of the tax coffers." Do you agree with Stephen Hawking's view?
- Give an account of the factors which led to the development and decline of the port of Liverpool.
- The election of Nelson Mandela eliminated apartheid. True or false?
- Describe the character of Piggy in *Lord of the Flies*. Illustrate your answer by close reference to episodes in the novel.
- Advances in genetic engineering will generate excitement and fear. Describe the scientific basis of developments which lead to these emotions.

There are 6 key stages in analytical writing:

1 Choosing a title
2 Researching for relevant information
3 Planning
4 Writing
5 Presenting your work, including the use of quotes, sources and footnotes
6 Checking

Stage 1 Choosing a title

When you have a choice of titles, select the title which gives you the best opportunity to write coherently and relevantly. If possible choose a title which interests you, or on which you have already done some work. If you don't fully understand a title, or find it difficult to relate to your understanding of the subject, then either choose a simpler title or seek advice. Just because a title is long does not necessarily make it more difficult to write about.

Consider these titles:
a Assess the importance of trade unionism in this century.
b Consider the impact which the growth of flexible working practices has had on the relationship between employer and employed. How successfully have employers, employees and trade unions attempted to cope with this change?

Writing

What would you say was the chief difference between the two titles?

. . . .

. . . .

. . . .

For our view of the difference see under Stage 3 Planning (page 96).

Stage 2 Researching

Unless you are going to be content with regurgitating notes you have already been given, you will need to undertake some research for your essay. At its simplest level, research might just involve you in following up a few references to books or articles which you have been told to consult. Even here, however, there may be difficulties caused by a shortage of the recommended books, so you may have to discover other sources for yourself.

Some assignments require lots of research; developing research skills can, in fact, be the reason for setting the assignment. You will need to find books, articles, journals, information from companies, government bodies or other relevant organisations. You may also need to use CD Roms and the Internet.

Whatever the focus of your research, you will be able to save yourself a considerable amount of time if you know how to make the best use of a library and its contents: See Library and Research Skills (page 59), Key Reference Resources (page 65) and Book Skills (page 70).

Before you begin researching make sure you know what sort of an approach the title demands:

> analysis
> description
> explanation
> detailed commentary
> comparison
> evaluation

The recommended length (usually 500 to 2500 words) will indicate how much depth and detail will be expected. If your handwriting is of average size you will get about eight words to a line, and approximately 250 words to each side of A4 paper. If you wordprocess your assignment your presentation will be more compact.

Having studied the question, ask yourself,

"What exactly do I need to find out?"

Your research must be selective and clearly directed at the title.

> 6 Collect all the information first. If the task is in parts, underline the information you are going to use for the various sections in different coloured pens. 9

> 6 Assignments at college require a lot more work to relate the information to the question asked. 9

Stage 3 Planning

This is the vital stage at which you relate and link your ideas, together with what you have discovered during your research, to the title. Planning helps to clarify your thoughts.

In an analytical assignment, your plan should also reflect the balance you need between descriptive and analytical writing. The majority of marks in this type of assignment will come from the analysis but you need to describe the content of the topic you are analysing. This should be sufficient for your analysis to make sense to the reader but you should not spend too much time on description, leaving too little time for analysis.

Construction is as important as content.

Why plan? Planning an assignment is as important as drawing up plans for a building. It ensures that your finished product has firm foundations, meets your requirements, and will stand up to critical scrutiny.

Planning

- Ensures that you stick to the point
- Organises your work in a coherent way
- Makes you think about priorities
- Saves time
- Prevents your writing from being a series of unconnected paragraphs
- Gives the reader a clear sense of direction. This makes your work much easier to read

The writing should be based on the title and not be just a replica of notes.

Remember: The person who marks your work will not wish to read all you know about a subject; instead she or he will want to see that you have been able to understand the title, and to relate your knowledge to the question being asked.

Compare these 3 different methods of planning for the following title: "Public transport is more socially equitable, and makes more efficient use of scarce resources." Comment on this view by referring to several methods of transport.

Method 1

Public transport does let some people, eg. OAP's, travel cheaply but particularly in the countryside buses and trains are slow and infrequent. If you need to travel a long way then flying is fastest. Concorde does use a lot of fuel and has been a great burden on the taxpayer, however it has enabled VIP's to get about very quickly which helps ordinary people in the long run.

Method 2

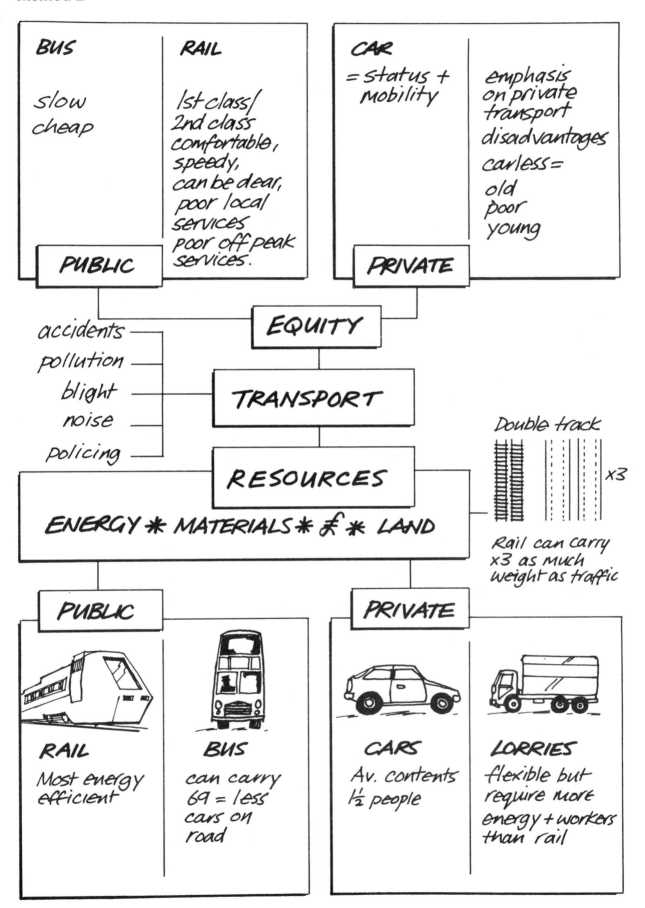

BUS

slow
cheap

RAIL

1st class/
2nd class
comfortable,
speedy,
can be dear,
poor local
services
poor off peak
services.

PUBLIC

CAR
= status +
mobility

emphasis
on private
transport
disadvantages
carless =
old
poor
young

PRIVATE

accidents
pollution
blight
noise
policing

EQUITY

TRANSPORT

RESOURCES

ENERGY * MATERIALS * £ * LAND

Double track

x3

Rail can carry
x3 as much
weight as traffic

PUBLIC

PRIVATE

RAIL
Most energy
efficient

BUS
can carry
69 = less
cars on
road

CARS
Av. contents
1½ people

LORRIES
flexible but
require more
energy + workers
than rail

Method 3

EQUITABLE ?

PUBLIC TRANSPORT		PRIVATE TRANSPORT	
PLUS POINTS	**MINUS POINTS**	**PLUS POINTS**	**MINUS POINTS**
Open to all. Concessions: OAPs, students	Rail can be expensive. Transport only to places on route. Lack of investment = poor services, routes closed, esp. in country areas	Mobility, flexibility. Easier on old & disabled (door to door)	29% households no car. Mobility according to income, not need. Tax subsidies to manufacturers, business users, lorries

RESOURCES

PUBLIC TRANSPORT		PRIVATE TRANSPORT	
PLUS POINTS	**MINUS POINTS**	**PLUS POINTS**	**MINUS POINTS**
Less capital needed than for new roads/ m.ways. More energy efficient: rail 166 passenger kms a litre of fuel, cars 16 passenger kms a litre of fuel	Capital costs seem higher — no hidden subsidies (policing, lighting)	Supports motor manufacturers	Accidents (cost to health service). Pollution. Noise, vibration. Stress (pedestrians, cyclists) Prime land for roads, car parks, runways.

WORTH MENTIONING!!

AIR Greater speed = more energy consumed

"Tell me how fast you can go and I'll tell you who you are."

Ivan Illich

SIDELINES & NOTES

" *Don't take hours over them. In the exam you only have 45 minutes.* "

" *Think them out first. Make sure you've included all the points asked for in the title. I leave long assignments to the weekend so I can spend a whole day on one thing.* "

" *Use diagrams where possible to make your work more interesting.* "

Method 1 (p93)

Although this shows some structured thinking it is more a summary than a plan and it does not present a quick visual reminder of the main elements of the essay.

Method 2 (p94)

This presents a visual structure of some of the key facts to be included in the essay. It also links some concepts under a single heading. However, some of the linkages in the structure appear complex and may confuse.

Method 3 (p95)

This structure comes closest to a hierarchy of concepts and should enable the writer to complete a logical progression. A reader is more likely to understand an essay if its structure can be clearly laid out.

Some titles provide you with a skeleton of a plan because they break down the topic into its chief elements. For example, title **b** in Stage 1 of this chapter (page 91):

> Consider the impact which the growth of flexible working practices has had on the relationship between employer and employed. How successfully have employers, employees and trade unions attempted to cope with this change?

This title immediately divides itself up into sections:
1 Definition/review of flexible working practices
2 Employees
3 Employers
4 Trades Unions

Stage 4 Writing

Your essay needs to be sufficiently well written so that
1 Your meaning is clear to the reader
2 You show you have understood the title
3 You show a coherent line of thought
4 You demonstrate that you can distinguish between the relevant and the irrelevant

Remember that the purpose of writing is for someone else to read your work. Therefore you should always bear in mind who will be reading it and whether they will find it easy to understand and enjoyable to read. As the purpose of writing at post-16 level is to show your knowledge of the subject, this must come through clearly.

The Fact Sheet Making Connections (page 99) gives you guidance about which words to choose to connect paragraphs and signal to your reader the direction your thoughts are taking.

Also remember that the teacher will be reading lots of essays on the same topic, probably in a short time. Make sure that your essay is easy to read, well structured and presented, so that your reader is not distracted from the content.

Compare the following opening paragraphs on the topic and write a comment about each in the sidelines.

What do you understand by the term "civilisation"? Do you consider that some ways of life are more civilised than others?

A Although modern man sets himself apart from other animals by saying that he alone can make fire, this is becoming less true. While almost every person can operate a lighter, or strike a match, how many members of the technical, Western World could, when given two pieces of wood and some natural fuel, build a cooking flame? Not many. Yet, to the "savage," "backward" tribes of primitive society, this is still a common skill.

B CIVILIZATION! It's strange to think you have just read a twelve letter word which was used as a pretence to exploit the Third World. It is a word which dictionaries strive to define, a word which professors profess about, a word which is supposed to put us above Stone Age Man and finally a word about which essays are written.

C In this essay I intend to explain the differences, as I see them, between the people in the western and third worlds. Civilization, as we know it, depends on all the aids of a modern technological society: machines, electricity, computers and above all silicon chips. I will demonstrate in this essay however, that this is far from being the case in the underdeveloped world. I will consider whether this means that people outside Europe and the USA are therefore less civilized. Here is a simple example to illustrate my point: in England we often see the ugly remains of a fire somewhere in the countryside, or perhaps near a campsite, but less developed peoples like the Aboriginals, take great care to spread out their ashes and to hide the remains of their fires. On the other hand, how well would tribesmen cope if they came to live in one of our big cities? Would they even be able to open a tin of beans? I doubt it.

D   Contrary to popular belief, being civilized DOES NOT depend on being technologically advanced, that is to say you do not need a television set, a motor car and other such silicon chip controlled luxuries. In fact you could even go so far as to say that, possibly, tribesmen and women are better off living in ignorance of these and other such things.

E   We are the so called civilised part of the world. We have television, space invaders, rockets to send men to the moon, and bombs that kill people but leave buildings intact. We wear expensive clothes and make-up to make us look beautiful so that we can be accepted in society. These expensive clothes are often made of animal skins and furs, and the make-up is often made of, and tested on, animals. Money is everything, and without it you can't get by. The rich get richer and the poor get poorer. Civilization has gone too far.

F   There are many different cultures in the world but many people in the western hemisphere have only one conception of "civilization", that being a highly educated society, well advanced in social development with a high level of equity. 'Primitive' people certainly lead a different way of life from ours, but does that imply that they are uncivilized?

Complete the table below by giving each extract a mark out of ten for each quality, and finish with a final comment.

Which of these extracts is apparently not on the point?

Which seems to address the title in the most structured way?

Which seems to address the title in the most interesting way?

Which shows the most potential, and makes you want to read on?

	Style	Structure	Clarity	Interest	Comment
A					
B					
C					
D					
E					
F					

FACT SHEET Making connections

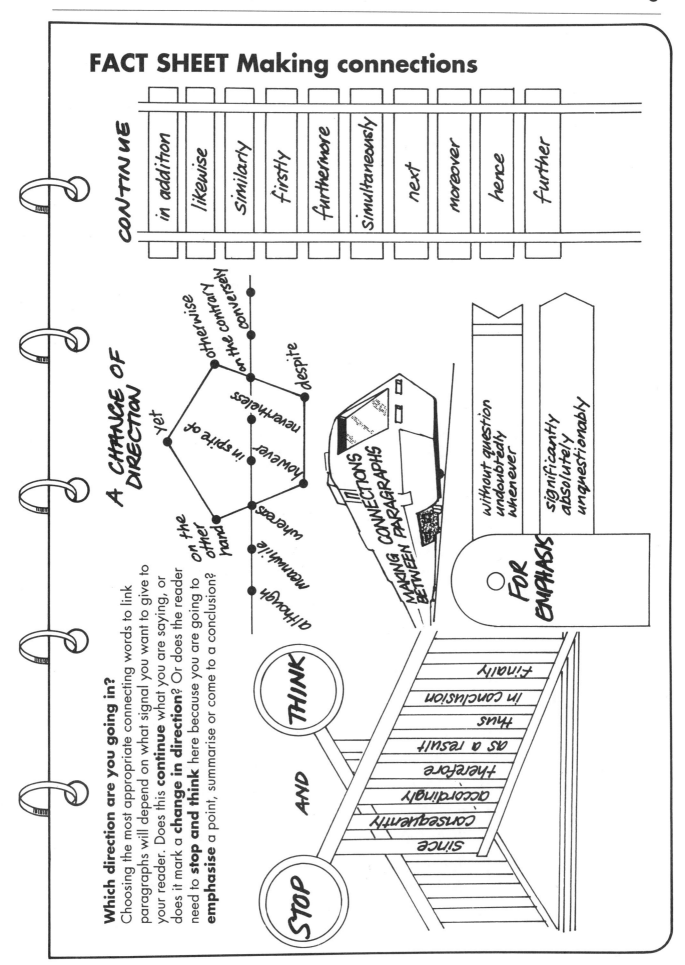

CONTINUE

in addition
likewise
similarly
firstly
furthermore
simultaneously
next
moreover
hence
further

A CHANGE OF DIRECTION

otherwise
on the contrary
conversely
yet
despite
nevertheless
in spite of
however
on the other hand
meanwhile
whereas
although

MAKING CONNECTIONS BETWEEN PARAGRAPHS

FOR EMPHASIS

without question
undoubtedly
whenever
significantly
absolutely
unquestionably

STOP AND THINK

since
consequently
accordingly
therefore
as a result
thus
in conclusion
finally

Which direction are you going in?

Choosing the most appropriate connecting words to link paragraphs will depend on what signal you want to give to your reader. Does this **continue** what you are saying, or does it mark a **change in direction**? Or does the reader need to **stop and think** here because you are going to **emphasise** a point, summarise or come to a conclusion?

Writing

Style

Plain and concise writing allows your reader to focus clearly on what you are saying. Flowery writing, and the use of clichés and jargon, distract attention from what you are saying, and instead call attention to the way you are saying it.

Flowery writing is writing that is too ornate and fussy for its purpose, for example

If I may be allowed to proffer an alternative opinion, albeit a personal one.

Clichés are phrases that are so over used that they have lost their original meaning and sharpness, and have now become a substitute for thought. (A cliché is literally a printers' term for words and phrases so often used that they were kept set in a block of metal type, instead of being made up each time from individual letters). Example:

He made sure no stone was left unturned.

Jargon (called "Gobbledygook" in America) is technical or specialised vocabulary which is often used unnecessarily, particularly to confuse, mislead or impress ordinary people.
Note in the sidelines what the following four pieces of jargon are actually saying.
Downsizing; negotiated departure; redundancy; work force imbalance correction

Slang is essentially oral and colloquial, and is therefore inappropriate for written work. Slang often originates as an escape from the plainness or occasional triteness of formal English. Slang can quickly become hackneyed through indiscriminate over-use; meaning and sharpness blur as the same words are regurgitated to save the effort of seeking more precise ones. Examples:

She kept going on about...He was dead lucky.

Mark the flaws in style in the following passage:

At this moment in time the necessity of maintaining and supplementing incrementally a nuclear deterrent is obvious to the man in the street. If we were to become embroiled in a confrontation situation with a potentially hostile nation state we would wish to have the capacity to pacify the situation by being able to deploy, at a moment's notice, a nuclear 'shot across the bows'. In this day and age gunboat diplomacy is obsolescent, and we should feel naked without the presence of our nuclear shield.

> *Science assignments require little style but they do require ordered sequence - introduction, a number of points covered in single paragraphs, and a conclusion.*

> *Get down to the point and don't waffle.*

Avoid using "etc." in your essays; it is vague and suggests you are not quite sure of what you are writing about.

Stage 5 Presentation

The use of primary and secondary sources

It is important to tell your reader what evidence, or sources, you are basing your arguments on, for example, an art student will refer to particular paintings while a geographer may cite physical locations. There are two types of source material: primary sources and secondary sources.

Primary sources (or evidence) are the raw materials of the subject. They are the originals. Examples of primary sources would be:

- an extract from *Pride and Prejudice* for an essay about Jane Austen
- an extract from the *Domesday Book* for an essay about Norman England
- census figures for an assignment on population
- a painting by Picasso for research on modern art
- experimental results for a scientific report

Secondary sources are the interpretations, commentaries, essays and books written about the primary sources. Each new generation of scholars and writers interprets the primary sources in a slightly different way. Examples of secondary sources would be:

- a critical commentary on Jane Austen's novels
- a historian's view of the Norman Conquest
- a demographer's analysis of population trends
- an art critic's interpretation of Picasso's work
- an article in *New Scientist* about some recent experimental results

Read the following extracts and note beside each whether they are a primary or secondary source:

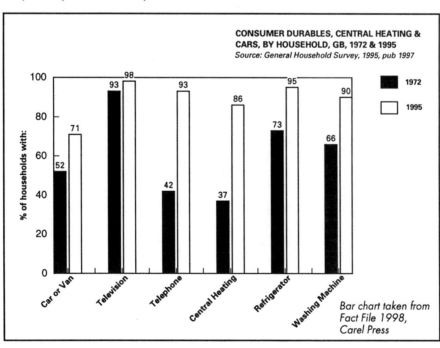

CONSUMER DURABLES, CENTRAL HEATING & CARS, BY HOUSEHOLD, GB, 1972 & 1995
Source: General Household Survey, 1995, pub 1997

Bar chart taken from Fact File 1998, Carel Press

'Chairman Mao,' as we always called him, began to impinge directly on my life in 1964, when I was twelve. Having been in retreat for some time after the famine, he was starting his comeback, and in March of the previous year he had issued a call to the whole country, particularly the young, to 'learn from Lei Feng.'

Lei Feng was a soldier who, we were told, had died at the age of twenty-two in 1962. He had done an awful lot of good deeds – going out of his way to help the elderly, the sick and the needy. He had donated his savings to disaster relief funds and given up his food rations to comrades in the hospital.

Lei Feng soon began to dominate my life. Every afternoon we left school to 'do good deeds like Lei Feng.' We went down to the railway station to try to help old ladies with their luggage, as Lei Feng had done. We sometimes had to grab their bundles from them forcibly because some countrywomen thought we were thieves. On rainy days, I stood on the street with an umbrella, anxiously hoping that an old lady would pass and give me an opportunity to escort her home – as Lei Feng had done. If I saw someone carrying water buckets on a shoulder pole – old houses still did not have running water – I would try unsuccessfully to summon up the courage to offer my help, although I had no idea how heavy a load of water was.

Jung Chang, *Wild Swans*, Harper Collins, 1991

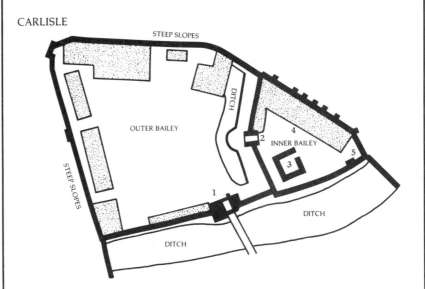

CARLISLE

The castle, founded c.1093 by William II, was ordered to be rebuilt by Henry I in 1122, and in 1135 was ceded to the Scots. It was probably rebuilt with masonry by King David and after its surrender to Henry II in 1157 it remained a Crown possession. Between 1173-1461 it was besieged nine times by the Scots but only taken once, in 1216 by King Alexander II who repaired and strengthened it.

M J Jackson, *Castles of Cumbria*, 1990, Carel Press/Cumbria County Library

Gender	Height (cm)	Weight (kg)
F	126.3	25.4
F	126.3	35.7
M	127.6	25.4
M	132.7	30.2
M	150.3	44.3
M	126.5	25.8
F	128.6	27.2
F	128.2	23.7
F	145.7	56.6
M	135.7	31.8
F	126.0	29.8
F	124.6	30.0
M	153.5	44.7
M	149.1	37.0
F	143.8	36.9
F	127.7	27.0
F	128.2	26.3
M	138.7	36.0
F	136.3	30.2
M	123.0	24.3

A survey of the heights and weights of 20 children

This information was collected as part of an investigationinto the relationship between height and weight.

Source: MRC/NIAS 1997

M = Male

F = Female

Women are told from their infancy and taught by the example of their mothers, that a little knowledge of human weakness, justly termed cunning, softness of temper, 'outward' obedience and a scrupulous attention to a puerile kind of propriety, will obtain for them the protection of man.

Mary Wollstonecraft, *The Vindication of the Rights of Women,* 1792

> One evening of late summer, before the nineteenth century had reached one-third of its span, a young man and woman, the latter carrying a child, were approaching the large village of Weydon-Priors, in Upper Wessex, on foot. They were plainly but not ill clad, though the thick hoar of dust which had accumulated on their shoes and garments from an obviously long journey lent a disadvantageous shabbiness to their appearance just now.
>
> Thomas Hardy, *The Mayor of Casterbridge*, 1886

A personal experience, or one of your family's, may seem to have a connection with an essay title, but only rarely will the experience be both relevant and appropriate to include. In the following example, however, a student has made good use of personal experience as an introduction to some more general points on prejudice.

My grandfather recalls his boyhood in the East End of London, where different types of cultures lived together. It was a poor, immigrant area, near the docks. Immigrants came over to seek a better life and they brought with them foreign habits, clothes and language. There was obvious resentment from the local people: local youths would attack the children of immigrant families, who in turn formed gangs to protect themselves.

This resentment expressed itself in a larger way in the rise of the fascist movement, which exploited cultural differences for political purposes.

The use of quotations

It is best to keep quotations, from both primary and secondary sources, short. The person who is going to read and mark your work will know both the primary and secondary sources and will be interested in the comments you make about the quotations, and in how well you have related your quotes to your arguments. In a good assignment, the quotes form an integral part of the argument. In a poor one, the quotes stand out as ill-digested raw materials.

Short quotes, of up to a line in length, should simply be put in quotation marks. Longer quotes should begin on a new line at 4cm in from the margin. You use single spacing for longer quotes even if you have used double spacing for the main body of the writing.

For both quotes and references you should acknowledge the source

Tawney, Religion and the Rise of Capitalism

Summary: Choose appropriate, brief quotes, and explain clearly how they are relevant to the point you are making.

Bibliography and references

As well as using quotes in your essay you should name the sources you have read, or referred to, in the bibliography (list of resources) at the end of your essay.

The advantages of a bibliography are:
• You can return to any of the sources at a later date because you have the exact reference at hand.
• Your reader can see how widely you have read.
• Your reader can check your evidence or sources.

Note

1 Author's name, with the surname first in block capitals, followed by the author's first name(s).
2 Title
3 The publisher and year of first publication (found on the back of the title page).

Example:

TAWNEY, Richard Henry, Religion and the Rise of Capitalism, OUP, 1926

Footnotes (For University level essays only.)
Footnotes are used in more detailed and scholarly essays for two purposes:
1 To give a reference to a book quoted, or referred to, in your essay:
   From Plan to Market, World Development Report, 1996 p66
2 To give interesting or additional details which are not sufficiently important or relevant to go into the main body of the text.

Footnotes should be numbered and can either appear at the bottom of each page, which is easiest for the reader, or in a list at the end.

Appearance of the finished assignment

If a piece of work looks well presented, in other words it is neat, clearly written and well paragraphed, then whoever is reading or marking it starts off with a favourable impression.

SIDELINES & NOTES

Thomas Carlyle spent three years writing the first volume of The French Revolution. He lent it to John Stuart Mill, whose housemaid mistook it for waste paper and burnt it. Carlyle had to start again.

Ernrest Hemingway lost his first novel on a train journey from Paris to Rome, while T E Lawrence left his book, Seven Pillars of Wisdom, in the refreshment room of Reading station.

' *After I've finished writing an essay I know I should check it through but for some reason I just want to hand it in as soon as possible.* **'**

Wordprocessing

This gives a more professional appearance to your work, making it easier to read, and revise from. You should use double spacing, and print on one side of the page only. This will allow space for additions later on the printed version and for notes and corrections from your teacher. A margin of about 4cm allows the person marking your work to make marginal comments.

Wordprocessing allows you to edit and improve your text. If acceptable to your assessor, you may be able to submit your work on disc. See also page 125

Keep a copy

If an essay has taken some time to write, then it is worth keeping a copy just in case the original gets lost. You could either make a carbon copy or photocopy a typed or handwritten essay. As a second best you could keep your rough draft or plan.

If you have used a wordprocessor, as well as saving your work you should have a back up disc and/or a second hard copy.

Stage 6 Checking

Many students are so relieved when they finish writing that they overlook checking, or persuade themselves it is not necessary. Some know they haven't done justice to the title, and would be embarrassed to read it through.

In fact checking is quickly done and allows you to ensure that your work is not marred by an obvious mistake, or made difficult to read by a slip of the pen. Spelling mistakes can be rectified if you have used a wordprocessor with a spellchecker. You will still, however, have to check for factual errors, style, omissions etc. Use the checklist on page 107 as a guide when writing and checking your work.

Feedback

When their work is returned, too many students look only at the grade or mark, and not at the comment. To benefit from the process of marking you should take careful note of the marginal and final comments. If there is something you do not understand then this is the best time to sort it out.

It is valuable to note down separately the comments made on your work, and then to make your own comment. Don't simply write "I must try harder" - that is too vague to be useful. Instead note one or two specific ways in which you could improve.

By filling in the Feedback Record Sheet on page 108 you will be able to learn from your mistakes, and to monitor closely your own progress. This is particularly important if you are on a continuous assessment course.

RECORD SHEET

Checklist for writing

Read through this checklist when you have chosen your title. Write the title on the right. Check off the points at each stage.

Titles

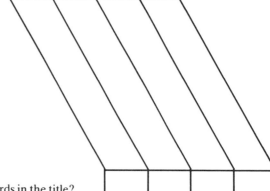

	Stage 1: **Choosing a title**	Have I identified the key words in the title?				
	Stage 2: **Researching**	Have I completed the necessary research?				
	Stage 3: **Planning**	Have I planned?				

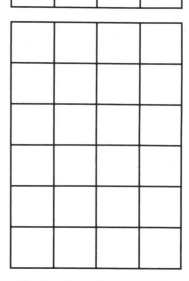

Stage 4: **Writing**	Have I written in the style required (analytical or factual)?
	Is what I have written relevant to the title?
	Is there a logical development and conclusion?
	Are my facts and quotations accurate?
Stage 5: **Presentation**	Have I quoted my sources?
	Have I written enough?
	Have I listed the books I have read, and referred to, in my bibliography?
Stage 6: **Checking**	Is each major idea developed in a separate paragraph?
	Have I avoided clichés, jargon & slang?
	Have I checked carefully for mis-spellings?
	Have I left any words out?
	Have I used punctuation properly?
	Have I kept a copy?

Writing

RECORD SHEET

Feedback

Title and date	Marker's comments	My comments

108   Strategies for Studying © Carel Press

17 Widening your vocabulary

As you read through this chapter, underline any unfamiliar words, jot down your guess at the meaning in the sidelines, then later check your guess in the dictionary. The word 'colloquial is used as an example below.

> *I jot down words I'm not sure about and then look them up later.*

Why?

Broadening your vocabulary will
- **make** you feel more self-confident in lessons and discussions
- **help** you to follow the thread of a complex argument
- **enable** you to select the shade of meaning you require
- **allow** you to select words which are appropriate in particular contexts, for example in either a formal or <u>colloquial</u> context ————
- **improve** your understanding of difficult books and articles
- **increase** your reading speed because you won't have to stop to puzzle out words, or look them up in a dictionary
- **help** you to avoid repetition in writing

Guess; not formal, casual
Check: to do with conversation, informal idiom or vocabulary

We can classify your vocabulary into two categories:
Active vocabulary: words that you know and use in a variety of circumstances
Passive vocabulary: words that you understand but would be unlikely to use
In order to broaden your vocabulary, you might transfer words from your passive to active vocabulary and add words to your passive vocabulary.

Which words?

You will only learn new words effectively when you need to know them. This is how you learned to speak originally. You should concentrate therefore on words which:
- will help your studies
- you meet in reading
- you will be able to use in notes, writing and discussions

Trying to learn lists of words copied from a dictionary or a magazine is to remove the point and context from learning. This is frustrating, time wasting and pointless.

Widening your vocabulary

How?

Context

The context (the sentence or paragraph in which the word appears) often provides clues to the meaning of an unfamiliar word. For example, you may not know the meaning of 'antecedent' but when you read it, you might be able to deduce part of the general sense of the word, though not its specific meaning:

> "The antecedent of this modern theory is to be found in an obscure book published in 1848."

The more frequently you meet a word in a variety of contexts, the clearer you will become about its precise meaning and connotations.

Dictionaries

Look up unfamiliar words in a good modern dictionary. You can hear words pronounced on the Concise Oxford Dictionary on CD Rom.

Personal dictionary

You can use a couple of pages at the back of your file, or in your exercise book, to make your own dictionary. By rephrasing the dictionary definition, and by writing your own sentence containing the word, you will help to fix its meaning in your mind.

Thesaurus

A thesaurus, or dictionary of synonyms, can be useful if you are seeking

- a particular shade of meaning
- a word that has slipped your mind
- a word to suit a particular context

(See page 65 for further details.)

Most word processing packages contain a thesaurus. If you are not sure that you have written the correct word, highlight it and click on the thesaurus. You will often find exactly the right word – and your work will be much better.

Reading

Wide reading of books, magazines and quality newspapers, will help to broaden your vocabulary. Particularly good are *The New Statesman, New Scientist, New Internationalist* and *The Spectator.*

Glossaries

Many books which make use of technical terms contain a glossary to explain these words.

Active listening

Listening attentively in lessons, and to serious items on television and on the radio, will help you to become aware of how words are used.

Warning

If, however, you remain unsure of the meaning of a particular word, do not use it simply hoping to be right. Students always do better in their studies when they write or talk knowledgeably about their subject.

FACT SHEET Prefixes and suffixes

A prefix is a group of letters which when put at the front of a word, or word stem, changes the meaning. Suffixes are word endings. Knowing the meaning of some prefixes and suffixes will help you to deduce the general meaning of many words.
Below is a list of prefixes in alphabetical order. The meaning of each is given. Give an example of the use of each.

Prefix	Meaning	Example	Prefix	Meaning	Example
Ab	away from, out of	*abscond*	In	not	....
Ad	to	....	Infra	below, beneath	....
Ante	before	....	Inter	between, among, across, through	....
Auto	self, by one's self	....	Mis	wrong, ill	....
Bene	well	....	Omni	all	....
Bi	two, twice	....	Ortho	straight, upright, true	....
Cata	below, down	....	Palaeo	old, ancient, prehistoric	....
Co	together	....	Per	through, across, by means of	....
Com (con)	together, with	....	Philo	love	....
Contra	against	....	Poly	many	....
De	below, down	....	Post	after	....
Dia	through, across	....	Pre	before	....
Dis	apart, removal	....	Pro	before, in front of	....
En	in, into, cause to be	....	Re	again, repeated	....
Epi	on	....	Retro	backwards, after, behind	....
Ex, E	away from, out, of	....	Sub	below, under, part of	....
Hetero	unlike	....	Tele	far, distant	....
Homo	same	....	Trans	across, through	....
Hyper	over, in excess	....			
Hypo	below, down	....			

On a separate piece of paper you could now group these prefixes according to meaning, for example by listing those which mean down or below.

Certain suffixes indicate the function of words:
-tion = a noun
-ly = an adverb
-ful = an adjective

18 Dealing with data

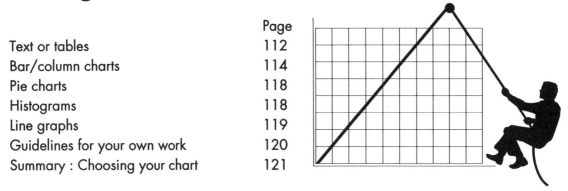

Well presented data enhances your work and helps to express complex ideas in a simple format. It is important, however, to know when to use a table or graph and which type to use.

In this chapter we will look at a range of data presentation techniques. You are likely to be familiar with all of them but you must be aware of the strengths and weaknesses of each so that you can interpret data accurately and present your own data effectively.

Attractive tables and graphs can hide some poor data-gathering techniques. The value of the data is only as good as the methods used to obtain it. Your tables or charts need to highlight the points you wish to make without either distorting the data or drawing conclusions which the data cannot support.

Text or tables?

Read this newspaper article.

United tops World's Richest Clubs League

Manchester United is the richest club in the world according to a new survey by accountants Deloitte and Touche, and *FourFourTwo* magazine. They dwarf their Spanish and Italian rivals. United has a turnover of £87.9 million, while the nearest English club, Newcastle United has only £41.1m despite the best efforts of some of its notorious directors. Liverpool, whose glory days are well in the past, just makes it into the top ten with a turnover of £39.2m.

United's financial muscle is 50% more than the great Spanish teams. Barcelona, which refuses to demean itself by having sponsored shirts, turns over £58.9m, with Real Madrid narrowly behind at £55.7m. Juventus are the biggest Italian club at number 4 in the table with £53.2m, while Milan is at number six with £47.5m and Internazionale scrapes in at number 10 with £39.1m. The remaining spots go to Germany with Bayern Munich (no. 5, £51.62m) and Borussia Dortmund (no. 7, £42.2m).

Numbers can spoil the flow of text and it is often difficult to get all you might from the data. For example can you find out quickly from the text above which club had the sixth biggest turnover? The text is accurate and informative, but the use of a table would have presented the information in a more succinct and organised way allowing the writer to focus, in the text, on informative details and perspectives.

	Club	Country	Turnover £m
1	Manchester United	England	£87.9m
2	Barcelona	Spain	£58.9m
3	Real Madrid	Spain	£55.7m
4	Juventus	Italy	£53.2m
5	Bayern Munich	Germany	£51.6m
6	Milan	Italy	£47.5m
7	Borussia Dortmund	Germany	£42.2m
8	Newcastle United	England	£41.1m
9	Liverpool	England	£39.2m
10	Internazionale	Italy	£39.1m

Turnover of the world's top ten football clubs
Source: survey by accountants Deloitte &Touche, and FourFourTwo magazine, 1999

However, text is best for data when numbers are all loosely related. Here is an article on privatisation of gas supplies to homes.

Lots of hot air as gas market opens up

Gas is being sold door-to-door these days and before long the entire country will resound to sales patter as competition hots up. From next Monday, half a million people in Dorset and the former county of Avon will have a choice of fifteen gas suppliers. They join half a million people in Devon, Cornwall and Somerset, who have had competition since April 1996. Next month a million in Kent and East and West Sussex will join them.

By the end of 1998, the whole country is supposed to have a choice of supplier.

Under competition in Devon, Cornwall and Somerset, gas prices have fallen 15-20 per cent below those of British Gas, according to regulator Ofgas. That saves roughly £45-£60 on the average domestic bill.

It would be impossible to put the different data in this article into any single table or chart.

Look through your own notes and see if you can find an example of text which contains lots of data which would be better in a table or chart.

Tables

Most data comes in tables. Before you use data you need to judge how reliable it is. Ask yourself questions like:

Who collected it?

When was it collected? Is it up-to-date?

How was the data collected?

Often tables in newspapers and textbooks do not give sufficient information for you to judge its reliability. Look at this data:

Typical cost of bringing up a child of secondary age
Source: What price a child – the School Years, Asda, 1996

Pocket money	£970
Christmas/birthdays	£1,835
Birthday parties/outings	£150
Additional purchases	£500
Eyecare/glasses	£0
Clothes including uniform	£1,586
Private education	£0
School equipment/ bags	£82
School meals/ packed lunch	£1,200
School trips & pocket money	£590
Sports gear	£660
Sports activity/viewing	£1,852
Own TV/ video	£500
Telephone in room	£0
Redecoration/study equipment	£230
Grooming/hairdresser	£270
Toiletries inc. shaving	£350
Sanitary protection	£110
Entertainment/ eating out	£1,981
Travel/petrol	£162
Outings eg theme park/zoo	£400
Food bill	£5,460
UK/foreign holiday	£855
Electricity	£418
Contents insurance	£165
Life insurance	£964
Increased mortgage	£8,962
TOTAL	**£30,252**

Dealing with data

The data represents a serious attempt to cost the bringing up of a child. Now imagine you are about to use the data in a project on the cost of living. Think about some of the questions you would want answered if you needed to work out the reliability of the data.

Who collected it? ASDA stores - does this affect your confidence in the data? Why or why not?

. . . .

. . . .

When was it collected? In 1996. Do you know the age of any child on which the data is based? They could be 11 in 1996 or 16 in 1996. In the end the figures are added together to represent the sum over the 11 - 16 years. How does this make a difference?

. . . .

. . . .

How was the data collected? By questionnaire? Interview? How were the questions phrased? Why does this matter?

. . . .

. . . .

Who was asked? - all shoppers at ASDA? A random sample across the population? A selected sample? How many people were involved? What if the child on which the data was based was from a big family? That might make things cheaper. Would the data be different for an only child? How might the sample affect the results?

. . . .

. . . .

Just because some questions about data collection cannot be answered doesn't necessarily make the data useless. However, if you use the information you must be aware of limitations and let your readers know you are aware.

Which data in the table do you think is most reliable? Which is least reliable? Give reasons.

. . . .

. . . .

. . . .

. . . .

Bar/column charts

These are sets of values plotted to create either a group of bars (horizontal plot) or a group of columns (vertical plot), generally with a space between each bar or column. Graphs with bars or columns are often used to show quantities, especially when different things are being compared. Because you see values side by side, it is easy to see which bar is longest or which column is tallest. They are useful for stressing the **differences between items at the same point in time**. One or more data series may be plotted on the same chart.

For example look at the bar chart on the next page showing the amount we spend on different foods.

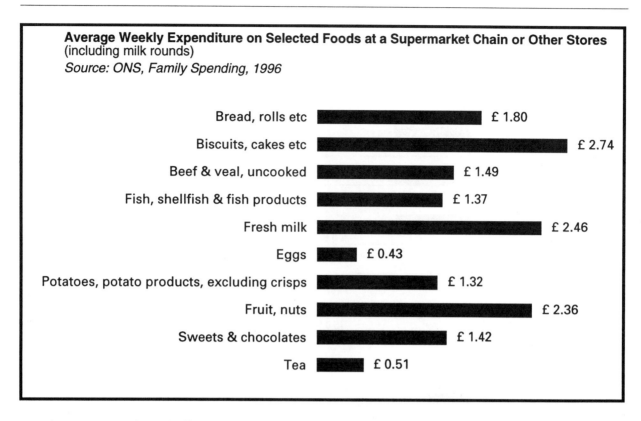

Bar charts are simple and effective but they can be made more attractive by making them into a **pictogram.** This is useful where you need to make a strong visual impact and when absolute accuracy is not necessary. Pictograms are often used in newspapers and on television, where there is a need to make figures instantly interesting and informative to a lot of people.

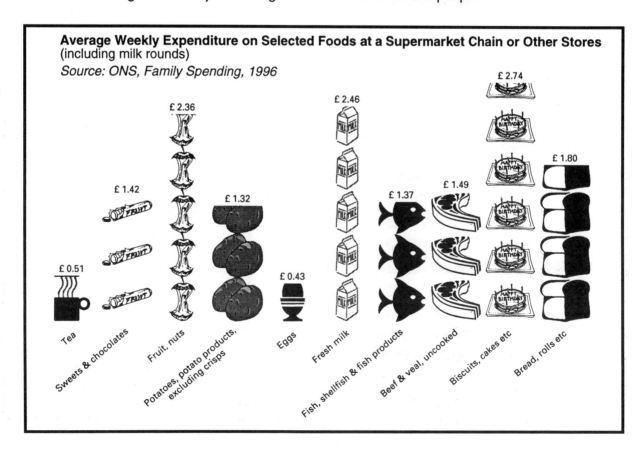

Dealing with data

The bar chart can be made to say more by making it a bit more complicated.

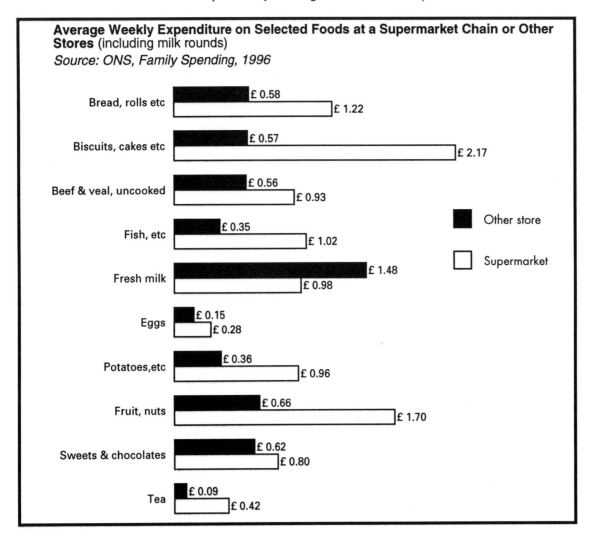

The same information can be presented as a **mirrorgraph**

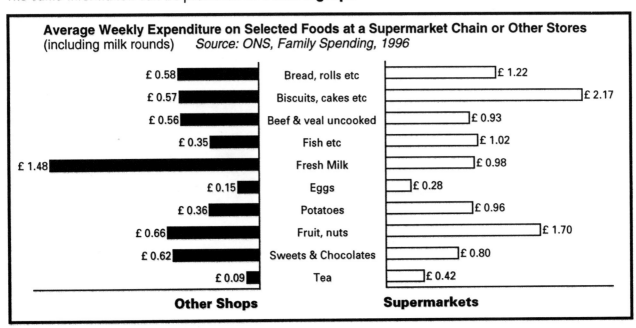

Another way of presenting the data is as a **stacked bar** with different foods occupying a length

Average Weekly Expenditure on Selected Foods at a Supermarket Chain or Other Stores (including milk rounds)
Source: ONS, Family Spending, 1996

Other Shops £5.42

Supermarkets £10.48

£ 0.00   £ 2.00   £ 4.00   £ 6.00   £ 8.00   £ 10.00

Tea   Sweets/chocolates   Fruit, nuts   Potatoes etc   Eggs

Bread, rolls   Milk   Fish   Beef & veal, uncooked   Biscuits, cakes etc

Make a single stacked bar chart below for the combined expenditure on these foods of £15.90
A convenient length for a bar is 15.9cm. Each centimetre is then equivalent to £1, each millimetre
being 10p. The outline of the bar has been drawn for you below.

Average Weekly Expenditure on Selected Foods at a Supermarket Chain and Other Stores (including milk rounds)
Source: ONS, Family Spending, 1996

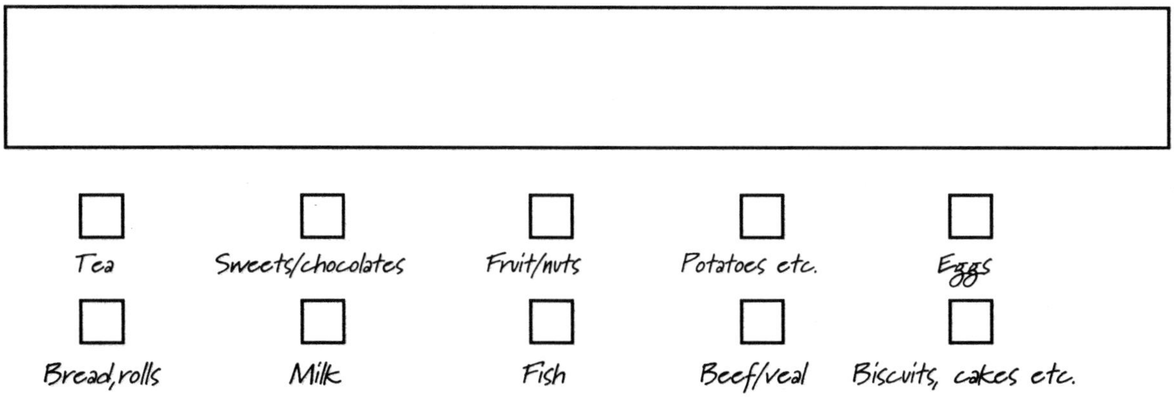

Tea   Sweets/chocolates   Fruit/nuts   Potatoes etc.   Eggs

Bread, rolls   Milk   Fish   Beef/veal   Biscuits, cakes etc.

A single stacked bar chart is a variation on a **pie chart**.

Pie charts

In a pie chart the data is shown as a sector of a circle. The size of the sector is in proportion to the category it represents. Pie charts are useful for showing the **relative importance of different parts in relation to the whole thing.**

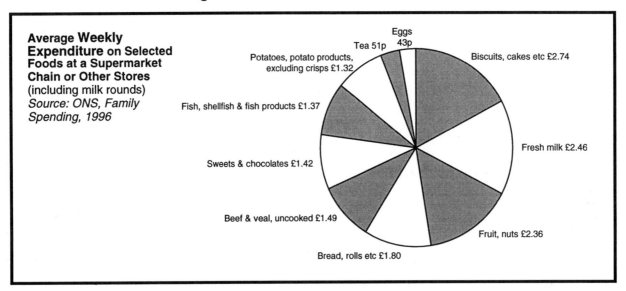

Average Weekly Expenditure on Selected Foods at a Supermarket Chain or Other Stores (including milk rounds) *Source: ONS, Family Spending, 1996*

Eggs 43p
Tea 51p
Potatoes, potato products, excluding crisps £1.32
Biscuits, cakes etc £2.74
Fish, shellfish & fish products £1.37
Fresh milk £2.46
Sweets & chocolates £1.42
Beef & veal, uncooked £1.49
Fruit, nuts £2.36
Bread, rolls etc £1.80

The food expenditure data can be made into a pie chart. There are 360 degrees in a circle so
£15.90 = 360 degrees

£1 = 360 ÷ 15.90 or 22.6 degrees

10p = 2.26 degrees

You can use a protractor to make the segments of the pie. Start with the biggest amount, £2.74 on biscuits and cakes at 12 o'clock and work around from the biggest slice to the smallest. Alternatively you can work with your computer using a spreadsheet program such as DeltaGraph Pro or the spreadsheet module in ClarisWorks.

Histograms

When you want to **show how one thing changes** you can use a **histogram**. These look like column charts but with no spacing. They are used to show how the frequency of one value changes in relation to another. The horizontal scale of a histogram is a continuous series of values. In the example below the histogram shows how the number of drownings changes with age.

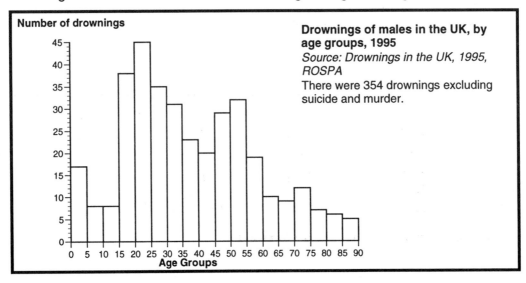

Number of drownings

Drownings of males in the UK, by age groups, 1995
Source: Drownings in the UK, 1995, ROSPA
There were 354 drownings excluding suicide and murder.

Age Groups

Line graphs

When the data is continually changing it is best to use a line graph. Trends and patterns show up on line graphs. You should use line graphs where you are trying to **interpolate** *or* **extrapolate.**

Interpolate: you make a measurement between the plotted points on a graph and on a graph line.
Extrapolate: you extend the graph to estimate a measurement which is beyond its plotted points.

Look at the data in the line graph below. It shows how the level of radioactivity changes with time in human kidneys.

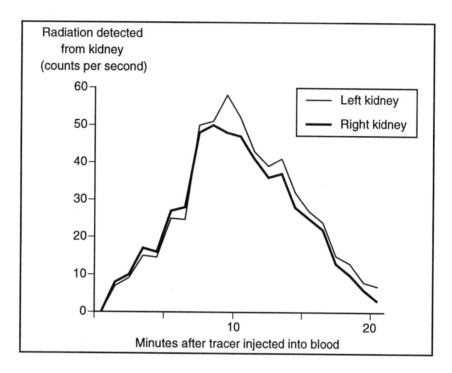

Doctors use this graph to check that the kidneys are working properly. They draw the graph using measurements of the radioactivity given off by the kidneys over time. This is done by infusing the patient's blood with a chemical compound containing a radioactive isotope. The kidneys then filter the radioactive traces from the blood to be excreted in the urine. Radioactivity in the kidneys is measured during the whole procedure. If the kidneys are working properly the radioactivity level rises as the chemical is filtered from the blood by the kidneys, then the radioactivity falls as the compound is flushed out of the kidneys to the bladder.

Interpolation: What is the radiation detected (in counts per second) 11 minutes after the tracer was introduced?

Left kidney .... Right kidney ....

Extrapolation: What do you think the radiation detected (in counts per second) will be after 30 mins?

Left kidney .... Right kidney ....

Guidelines for using charts and graphs in your own work

You may wish to include charts or graphs in your work. Graphing programs make this relatively easy.

The graphic must be **clear**. You must
- ensure that you are using the type of graph that will present the data correctly
- display the information clearly so that the data is easy to work on and readers are encouraged to think about the content of the chart
- provide both the broad picture and the fine detail
- help your readers to interpret the data
- clearly label the graph with the source and date of information
- label any important facts or information
- label the x and y axes on graphs
- always give a title
- include a key or scale where necessary
- avoid the temptation to use elaborate patterns or cross hatching simply because they are available on the computer program! Simplicity is a more difficult effect to achieve, yet it is more pleasing to the eye and makes the graphic easier to work with
- explain abbreviations

The graphic must be visually **appropriate** i.e.
- be the most suitable kind for the information it is displaying

A computer graphing program might offer 30 or more ways of displaying information. It is best to stick to the well known ones which are the most suitable for everyday educational use.

The graphic must be **accurate** i.e.
- be based on reliable information
- be faithful to the information being displayed
- present data fairly in context
- distortion (conscious or accidental) must be avoided

Be especially careful in presenting contrasting areas of magnitude in a graphical way

For example if a drawing of a £10 note measuring 8cm x 4cm represents a country's exports in 1998, and if the exports fall by half, the £10 note drawn to represent this should **not** be 4cm x 2cm. In doing this you would be representing a piece of one dimensional data (the fall in exports) by altering two dimensions in a two dimensional chart.

In other words, the area of the original £10 note is 32 square cm, if you halve both length and width you create a representation which is only 8 sq. cm - one quarter of the original, not half of it as should be the case.

Exports fall by half

Exports 1998 (Area = 32cm^2)

Exports 1998 (Area = 8cm^2)

Exports 1998 (Area = 16cm^2)

Summary: Choosing your chart

Whatever your subject or topic, if you have data to present you should consider using a chart or graph. With a carefully chosen graph you can present your information clearly, accurately and attractively. Some of the most useful types of chart are described here.

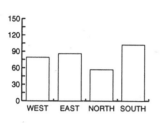

Bar Charts/Column Charts

These are sets of values plotted to create either a group of **bars** (horizontal plot) or a group of **columns** (vertical plot). Both charts are simple and clear ways of comparing values, sizes or amounts, usually at the same point in time. Because you see values side by side, it is easy to see which bar is longest or which column is tallest. One or more data series may be plotted on the same chart. You can also make 'stacked' bar/column charts where different qualities are show on the same bar/column.

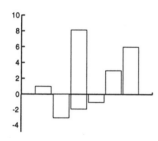

- Reverse column charts show negative as well as positive values, with columns which extend below the x axis. For example, a column chart showing monthly average temperatures might include some below zero values.

Useful for: Stressing the **differences** between items at the same point in time.
Examples of use: Gross Domestic Product of different countries; wages for different occupations.

Mirrorgraphs

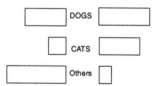

These are another type of bar chart. The labels of each bar can be placed centrally and the bars extend either side of these, almost like a reflection.
Useful for: Comparing two sets of data about a single set of subjects.
Examples of use: Comparing types of road vehicles recorded in the same place at different times.

Pictograms

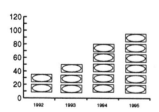

·Bar/column charts with pictures or images replacing the bars/columns.
Useful for: Making a strong visual appeal especially where it is not necessary to be absolutely precise. You will often see pictograms in advertising, newspapers or on TV, wherever figures have to be made interesting to a lot of people.

Histograms

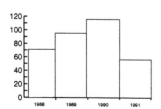

These are very similar to column charts, but have one important difference - the horizontal scale is a continuous series such as units of time. One or more data series may be plotted on the same chart.
Useful for: Viewing changes in values over a given period of time.
Example of use: Changes in average annual births.

Pie Charts

Circles which are divided into wedges (sectors). The size of the wedge is in proportion to the category it represents.
Useful for: Showing the relative importance of different parts in relation to the whole thing. Some computer programs will also allow you to separate the wedges to emphasise the differences
Examples of use: How people spend their leisure time; how a budget was divided up.

Line Graphs

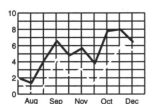

These show continuous change over a period of time or a number of events. Line graphs can be combined with bar graphs.
Useful for: Giving a strong visual impression if you have to plot a long series of data points. They can be used to compare trends by plotting more than one line in the same chart.
NB: If too many lines are used the chart can be confusing. If more than one line is used each line must look different and you will need to give a key.
Examples of use: Population figures for a country shown every decade for a century; sales over a period of time.

Scattergraphs

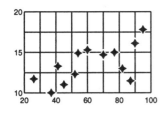

These can show the relationship between two variables.
Useful for: Revealing dependencies between variables - one of which may have an effect on another.
Examples of use: Showing the relationship between death rates and cigarette consumption.

Whichever type of graph you choose remember to think about its **title** carefully. It can be a good idea to sum up the graph's message in its title for example 'Overseas aid declining'. The **source** of the data should be given and the date when it was collected. The **axes** should always be clearly labelled.

Computers and Graphing

A computer can take much of the hard work out of creating graphs. There are many powerful programs available. Spreadsheets and integrated programs have built-in graphing options.

Recommended programs: The charting option within the spreadsheet of *ClarisWorks* deals with all the most common types of graphs, and also allows pictograms to be created. For serious charting, *DeltaGraph Pro* is a specialist program with an automatic chart adviser to suggest which type of chart would best suit your data.

Beware of the temptation to use a complicated type of graph when what you and your data really require is one of the basic ones. Also beware of creating a three dimensional graph on the computer when your data is only two dimensional. A little bit of restraint is called for with most computer programs! You want your chart to be attractive but above all you want it to be clear.

19 Computers

Used proficiently and with forethought, the computer can be a vital tool for learning. But it can still be a distraction if you become involved in the intricacies of a particular program, or the internet, rather than keeping your learning purpose and task in mind.

At first you may feel overwhelmed by what you need to learn but it becomes progressively easier as you grasp the basic functions and the return, in terms of efficient working, increases significantly.

Decide what you need to know

You already have more than enough to learn in the subjects you are studying, so you only need to know enough about computers and programs to speed up and help your work. Whilst the computers in the library or at college may have quite a wide variety of software, it is better to concentrate on using one or two programs properly, rather than knowing a little about several programs. Multi-purpose packages, such as ClarisWorks, which incorporate a wordprocessor, database, drawing & painting packages etc, will provide the vast majority of students with more than enough power and flexibility and will be quicker to learn than the more specialised programs which are full of features that you won't need to use.

Success with the computer

Most computers now conform to certain protocols. Software tends to follow standard approaches. Mouse operations, window functions and keyboard shortcuts are very similar between different types of programs and across different types of computers. This means that in terms of learning to use computers, it is more productive to learn these standard operations than to follow step by step instructions for a single program.

This is rather like learning to read a book. If you are given a completely new book, you know that you can expect the contents to be at the front,

Remember that the computer can both save and waste an awful lot of your precious time.

The best way to learn is to play. If you make a mess, you can just turn the computer off and start again.

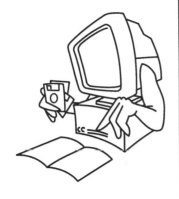

the index at the back and the chapters to run in numerical order. In other words you know how to read a book because you understand the structure of the book. This is the same with computer programs - if you understand the basics, you can go on to use a very wide range of programs.

Courses may be available at your place of study or perhaps at an evening class centre. Courses can be great, as long as they don't attempt to cover too much ground too quickly. Focus on your own purpose in learning during the course.

Computer manuals are not quite as indigestible as they used to be. However, as computers and programs have grown more powerful, there is more to explain in the manual. While few people could, or would want to, read a manual from cover to cover, using the manual is well worthwhile. At least read the introduction, scan the contents, note if there's a trouble-shooting section, and do read carefully any sections relevant to what you are about to do. Even that easiest to use, and friendliest of computers, the Apple Macintosh (which has useful, accessible guidance built in, encouraging you to get going quickly) will be much more use to you if you read about it first of all.

On screen help can be a useful alternative to the manual.

Web site discussions & help sites exist for many leading programs.

Program tutorials allow you to work through the possibilities of the program in a structured way on screen, with detailed instructions in the manual. If you are going to use a program a lot, this is a good investment of time and the sooner it's done the better, before pressures mount up on you. Some tutorials are contained only in the manual with relevant files on disc.

Computer books: Far from killing the book, the computer has generated a vast library of titles about itself. Usually these books are more user friendly than the manuals and they are often full of hints and tips. For example David Pogue's *Macs for Dummies* is fun to read as well as being useful. Some books also have free discs containing samples of programs and games.

Videos can provide an excellent insight to programs. Unfortunately, some are rather amateurish. The videos from MacAcademy/Windows Academy are well made. Videos are, however, expensive. Check to see if a library near you has any relevant ones.

Computer magazines: Amidst the pages of adverts there are sometimes useful guides to using programs. Look out for features on programs you are interested in.

Discussion: Compare the usefulness of computers and packages with fellow students. Which are the most user-friendly? What is your most useful tip for others?

Teach yourself! As long as you've got the time, it's fun to teach yourself, particularly as computers and programs get easier to use.

Wordprocessing

You don't need to be typist to use a wordprocessor, although this is yet another skill that would make you faster. A wordprocessor, such as the one in Claris Works, allows you to
* **enter** your written information via the keyboard
* **correct** spelling or typing errors easily and quickly
* **review** on the screen before printing
* **rearrange** the order of words, sentences and paragraphs
* **save** work and come back to it later to **revise** and **update**
* **copy** whole documents or sections into another document

A wordprocessor provides you with many facilities such as automatic page numbering, the ability to change tense or to change from capitals to small letters, emboldening, searching and replacing words or phrases. It will usually allow you to import graphs, or graphics, that you've created in another program.

How can they help you?
* You can present information neatly and in a suitable layout.
* You will be able to make necessary alterations or updates and immediately obtain a new copy without having to retype everything.
* You can rearrange, redraft or reorganise assignments without the chore of rewriting.
* You can print extra copies with ease.
* Most programs have spell checkers, which are useful but they won't do all the work for you - they can't cope with homophones (words which are pronounced the same, but differ in spelling or meaning). Many programs also have a thesaurus.
* Some programs even provide you with grammar checkers. However, because the English language is rich and complicated, these programs cannot be relied on. Some wordprocessors will spot more mechanical mistakes such as sentences that don't begin with a capital letter, or the consecutive repetition of a word.

Alternatives to typing
Scanning
If you are not a speedy typist, and you have to input a lot of text or data which is already printed or typed, then it may be better to scan the text, or data, using an OCR (optical character recognition) program, such as OmniPage. The quality of the printed original will affect the result, it may be very accurate but there may also be some hard to spot errors.

Voice control
Voice recognition software, by which you speak to, rather than type into, the computer, might be a help to slow typists working out of earshot from others. They are not as accurate as a good typist but might be worth

SIDELINES & NOTES

It's easier, and less tiring, to check work in hard copy rather than on screen.

I find a word-processor superb for writing essays. I still make a plan on paper but then, instead of having to write, re-draft and finally produce a best copy, I can type the essay into the computer, rearrange, add, delete and correct until I'm satisfied.

If you're used to wordprocessing then you may need to practise with pen and paper for the exams.

A radio programme about computers in the mid 1980s announced that the forthcoming generation of computers would be voice controlled, and we'd be able to wave goodbye to the keyboard. An earlier prediction from experts was that by 1985 school pupils would be carrying computer notebooks in place of pencil cases and notebooks.

'A student doing her dissertation was complaining that she could not find any material on her subject and that the librarian had been unable to help. I put in two keywords into a database and instantly found 33 references. This took less than five minutes while she had been looking for several months.' – Bob Sapey

considering. Unfortunately such programs aren't really capable of handling tapes from interviews because they have to learn to recognise one voice.

Importing from e-mail or web sites
Obviously you can import material direct from these two sources, but you must be aware of the distinction between quotation (with the source clearly acknowledged) and plagiarism (passing off someone else's work as your own).

Databases

A database is a vast store of information about a particular topic or topics. Databases allow information to be extracted easily and rapidly because they are capable of accessing and sifting through vast amounts of information very quickly. They do this by looking for keywords and cross referencing. If you ask the right question in the right way, you will get the answer you require.

Databases are capable of performing, very quickly, tasks that would otherwise take you a long time. More importantly, they can perform tasks that you would otherwise not consider worthwhile.

You will come across databases used as indexes to:
• books and periodicals in a library
• abstracts (summaries) from technical journals
In these two cases, the databases do not contain the information you seek but provide you with the means for finding it.

Consider these tasks:
Case 1: compiling a list of all the books concerned with computers in education published since 1998. This would be a very time consuming task. You would have to match all the book references to *Computers* with those of *Education* and identify those books which are in both lists. A database could provide you with this information instantaneously.
Case 2: compiling a list of references to articles on a particular topic, published in a specialist journal since 1995. This situation would at the very least require you to read the list of contents of each journal since 1995. A well structured database should give you the information you require in a matter of minutes or even seconds.

You might find it useful and time-saving to set up your own database of key information. If you are getting information through a questionnaire or have several sources of information for a project, your own database can be very handy. However, to make a success of this, you do need to invest the time in learning to use the database.

Limitations: It is important to find out the extent of the data held on a database. For instance, does the library database hold information only on books and journals purchased after a certain date or held at a particular branch? It may be that the database only gives the titles of books and journals and does not have information on what is stored within them. Other databases may be limited to publications from a particular country or countries. In each case you may still find the search for references useful, but if you know its limitations, you will not be deceived into believing it to be perfect.

Ask at your library to see what database facilities they provide. (For more information on library databases see page 61)

The World Wide Web

The aspect of the internet which students will probably use most is the world wide web, which is a type of super database. The internet has been described as like having the entire contents of the British

Library in your living room, but without a catalogue, and with an extra four pantechnicons of material arriving every day on your doorstep.

The web gives you access to a mass of information from across the world for the price of a local phone call. The web is becoming essential to a large number of organisations in terms of their PR communication. Therefore, there is a lot more information available directly from the source, albeit limited to one viewpoint. The web can provide, for example, government guidance papers and press releases which otherwise have a restricted paper circulation. In the field of research the web is an important means of publication. Many people are putting abstracts of academic papers on the web and there are many online journals.

However unless the subject you are studying is at the cutting edge of change, or very topical or involves the latest technology, then the web is probably not the best place to find and absorb the *essentials* of most subjects.

Just because material is on the web, doesn't necessarily mean it's the most up-to-date – it depends how recently the site was updated. It also doesn't necessarily mean that the information is accurate. Because the web is rather anarchic, there is simply no editor checking and selecting information for you. Anyone can add information, unproved theories or deliberate nonsense. And, of course, the web is increasingly the target of advertising, which finances the search engines. The web can be useful, and motivating, but should not be your only port of call.

Here are some useful sites:
JANET – the **Joint Academic Network**– hosts 2,303 subject discussion groups in higher education involving some of the leading academics. http://www.mailbase.ac.uk/

SIDELINES & NOTES

If you want to learn how to use the internet you could go to a cyber café, where you can pay for half an hour's tuition. For a regularly updated list of cyber cafés and internet access points in 113 countries see www.netcafeguide.com You could also try the public library.

' *Make sure you type the web address correctly – even a missing dot will stop you finding it.* '

To search for an exact phrase put quotation marks round it.

For news, today's speeches and to join in e-mail discussions started by the prime minister see the web site of **10 Downing Street** www.number-10.gov.uk/index.html (The site is slow due to the graphics)

It is possible to spend a lot of time following a trail to something that sounds interesting, only to find that the end of the trail is an advert for a book or magazine. So it is essential to learn where there are sites of value to you and keep those addresses, as 'bookmarks', so that you can return to them from time to time.

You could try some of the following sites for interest and information:
The Science Museum www.nmsi.ac.uk
Edinburgh University's World-wide earthquake locator is constantly up-dated www.geo.ed.ac.uk/quakexe/quakes
The Louvre www.louvre.fr
Learn Spanish on-line with the Spanish Institute (Instituto Cervantes) http://cvc.cervantes.es
HM Treasury   http://www.hm-treasury.gov.uk/
British Standards Institution www.bsi.org.uk
Tour de France www.letour.fr This official site is bi-lingual
Foreign & Commonwealth Office Travel Advice www.fco.gov.uk/
Tourism Concern (the pressure group for fair, sustainable and responsible tourism) www.gn.apc.org/tourismconcern

Many campaign groups use the net to keep their supporters informed. Two sites give an overview of many of these:
The Institute for Global Communications http://www.igc.apc.org
One World Online http://www.oneworld.org

For more sites see *Key Organisations* (Carel Press). Please remember that web site names do change from time to time, and the ones given here were correct at the time of going to press.

Search Engines

Using a search engine such as

Yahoo	www.yahoo.com **or** http://www.yahoo.co.uk
AltaVista	www.altavista.digital.com
Infoseek	www.infoseek.com
HotBot	www.hotbot.com/
Lycos	www.lycos.com
Inference Find	www.inference.com/infind
Netfind	www.netfind.co.uk

allows you to type in a key word or name and the engine searches and finds the web pages for you. These search engines scan untold numbers of web sites, so to avoid being overwhelmed by information make your request as specific as possible, for example, rather than requesting information on volcanoes, you might try Mount St. Helens.

Beware that some web sites have very large graphics or sound files which can cause your computer to freeze while downloading. The graphics may look attractive, but they take up enormous amounts of memory, and are therefore slow to download. It is possible to turn graphics off when downloading and just to receive text.

E-mail

Send messages, graphics, photos and computer files worldwide quickly, for the cost of a local phone call. E-mail can take just a few minutes, (longer if several computer networks have to be negotiated), but be careful to type the e-mail address exactly.

E-mail is an effective tool in encouraging co-operative learning groups at differert institutions. There are four ways of getting an e-mail address:
• **college/school**
Your college/school may provide you with an e-mail address.
• **internet service provider (ISP)**
Companies like AOL, Compuserve and Which? Online provide e-mail (as well as access to the world wide web) for a monthly fee.
• **free internet service providers**
Free e-mail and internet access was pioneered in the UK by Dixons (www.freeserve.net) but telephone technical support costs 50p a minute (free on-line). Freeserve also gives you 15Mb for your own web site, but you do need to use the service at least once every 30 days to maintain your presence. BT ClickFree (www.btclickfree.com or 0800 002 800) gives e-mail and web access, though not web space, for just the cost of a local call.
• **free e-mail**
Send and receive e-mails free from anywhere in the world (eg a cyber café or one of BT's new multi-media public kiosks). Providers sell advertising on their sites. To check on providers type free e-mail in the search box at www.yahoo.com. The largest provider is Microsoft's Hotmail (www.hotmail.com). These providers give no access to the world wide web.

SIDELINES & NOTES

E-mail was invented in July 1970

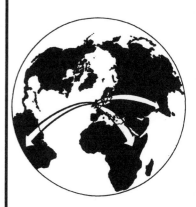

' *The trouble with having e-mail addresses with different servers is that you've got to check them all.* '

' *Computers are very useful for working with graphs and statistics.* '

Spreadsheets

Spreadsheets are for organising data (not just numbers) and presenting it in graphs, charts and tables. While databases organise information for you, almost like a very flexible electronic filing cabinet, spreadsheets are about statistical analysis. You enter your data into a grid with numbers down the side and letters across the top:

	A	B	C	D	E	F
1	Population	UK	England	Wales	Scotland	N Ireland
2	1981	56352	46821	2813	5180	1538
3	1994	58395	48708	2913	5132	1642
4	2001	59800	50023	2966	5143	1667
5	2031	62241	52435	2977	4998	1831

You can sort data alphabetically and numerically. Spreadsheets make the handling of lots of related facts and figures much easier.

One of the great advantages of spreadsheets is that they can do calculations for you. So when data changes the totals change, eg if you enter a simple formula in the example above to add C D E F to get B, then each time the population figure in one of the columns C D E or F changes, the total in B will alter at the click of the mouse.

' *I can't imagine how I managed without a spreadsheet* '

To assist you in learning

This use of computers in education is often known as CAL (Computer Assisted Learning). The main principle of using computers in learning is to enable the student to gain an insight into a specific topic that he or she could not gain using conventional methods.

One approach is programmed learning where you are presented with information followed by a question. If you answer correctly you move on to the next piece of work or possibly another question. If your answer was incorrect you are directed to some revision, followed by another question. Only when you prove yourself to be proficient in the area under study do you move on.

The same idea is employed by computers, which can handle this technique very effectively and add another dimension. They present interesting and varied information which can be animation, text, charts, or diagrams or any combination of these. The computer can make assessments of your progress and, as a result of your response, can make decisions on what it shows you or asks you next, pinpointing any shortcomings in your understanding. Remember though, that in assisting you in your learning, the computer is only as good as the software you use. Such programmed learning is especially well suited to factual or mechanical skills (eg using a typing tutor).

It's worth being aware of what computers are not suited to. They cannot help you to decide what you need to learn next as each individual will have different needs in this respect. So you must take responsibility for your own learning and not defer to the CAL package for this. The CAL package should be treated as a resource or tool, not as a tutor.

Computers make good learning aids because they have the ability to:
- work very quickly
- produce diagrams and charts
- animate pictures
- repeat monotonous procedures over and over again without becoming bored or inconsistent

Computer programs for education usually fall into one of the following categories:
- structured reinforcement
- modelling and simulation
- games and role play

Structured reinforcement

This usually concerns the learning of facts or information through repetition. For example, you might use this in learning spelling or French vocabulary or the periodic table etc.

Modelling and simulation

A simulation or model is a representation on a computer of a physical situation. Its main purpose is to give you experience of interacting with something that in the real world would be dangerous, time consuming, or difficult. Examples would be:

- transpiration of water molecules from the surface of a leaf, which it is not possible to see
- the internal operation of a nuclear power station reactor, which it would be dangerous to see
- the rate of soil erosion from a hillside, which happens over many years

Such simulations usually allow the user to alter factors, observe the effect and make further changes. In some you might be asked to make judgments and enter your decisions into the computer and then observe the outcome. In this way you can see the effect of your decisions on the model and test theories at first hand. A book can only give one version, whereas the computer program can pose questions such as:

'. . . what would happen if?'

Conversely, by changing parameters (factors) and getting the computer to respond, you can investigate the model in a way which you could not do otherwise.

Games and role play

These programs usually enable individuals or groups to become involved in a situation in which each person's actions affect what is happening to others. Many programs in this category have been written for economics, for the teaching of such topics as:

- supply and demand
- running the British economy

It is interesting to note that even the Government uses programs written on the same lines to test their economic theories before putting them into practice.

A word of warning here - the program is only as good as the underlying model. If the model is faulty then the predictions will be too. Many governments have found this out to their cost. It is easy, for example, to write a program to make predictions. It is far more difficult to make predictions that will come true.

The first law of computing should be: Back up your work or lose it.

Some practical tips

- There are already a number of instances of authors losing chapters and even whole books, because of computer failure. These invariably occur when you haven't backed up your work. Save regularly, for example every twenty minutes.

- As you begin to build up quite a collection of back-up discs, a program such as *Catalogue*, which conveniently catalogues the contents of hard, floppy & Zip discs, and lets you quickly search for particular items, is very useful.

- If you work on more than one computer, perhaps carrying a disc from home to college, it is all too easy to find that you are working on

At all times remember to back up work, and to keep a record of where the latest version of your work is.

'*I print the date on all my draft documents, then I know which is the latest version*'

Two school pupils searching a CD Rom encyclopaedia for a project on former Manchester United footballer Eric Cantona found an entry on Eric the Red, and promptly downloaded and printed this. Task completed they then stuck it under a picture of the footballer.

The article, which they had not read, began 'In about AD 982 a brawny, red bearded Norseman named Eric set out from the Northwest coast of Iceland...'

different versions of the same document. You may have some extra work and corrections done on one version but not on the other, and vice versa. This is always infuriating and systematic use of a program such as *Synchronize* can prevent this happening. *Synchronize* will update files so that the latest version is in both places.

- Modern computers allow you to produce such a variety of visual effects that it's easy to get carried away with altering the appearance of your work instead of improving the quality of its content. Most assignments and essays can be presented effectively using a wordprocessing program without the necessity of using a desktop publishing program.

- Stick to just two or three fonts (typefaces), at most, in a piece of work - restraint looks professional. A jumble of fonts and special effects looks amateurish and distracting. Remember that the purpose of writing is to be read. Fonts such as Trinity, Times New Roman and Helvetica are widely used because they are easier to read than some more elaborate fonts. (You are now reading Futura Book, another clear font).

If you are handing in an essay for marking, remember that the examiner may have to read dozens and you will be making their work more difficult if you present your work badly. Badly presented work that is difficult to read will result in a lower mark.

- Generous margins, double spacing or increasing the space (known as leading) between lines aids reading and leaves room for your tutor to make comments and corrections.

The main part of this book is set out using a print size of 10.5 and a leading of 12.8. The large margin at the side leaves room for your comments and makes the lines of print shorter and easier to follow.

- Use a virus checker on any borrowed discs.

CD ROMs

CD ROMs make vast quantities of information readily available. They incorporate attractive features not available in books, such as video and commentary, interactivity and keyword searches. Many reference texts, dictionaries, encyclopedias etc are on CD ROM. But the amount of data you can get onto a CD ROM can be a problem and it has led some manufacturers to fill them with 'shovel ware' - ie material of little use which is shovelled onto them to fill up all those megabytes of otherwise empty space.

As with all resources, the key thing is deciding what is most appropriate for your needs. CD ROMs aren't a replacement for books. Both mediums have their strengths and weaknesses. For example, it is quite easy to scan a book to assess its coverage and relevance. This is more difficult with CD ROMs.

Whilst CD ROMs appear to be interactive, in reality, choices are tightly controlled, and sometimes, instead of engaging with the material, students become merely 'click happy'. There are some exceptions such as the voice recognition software for teaching languages which can judge your pronunciation as between 'tourist' and 'native' and allows you to go on endlessly practising and perfecting your accent.

It's easy to download information from a CD ROM to a wordprocessing program, and this has unfortunately led a few students to incorporate material from an encyclopedia directly into their own coursework. This is plagiarism, and can lead to serious penalties, especially if the work is to be assessed for a qualification. In reality the only person cheated is the student because no learning is likely to take place. Putting text from a CD ROM into your own words, on the other hand, is an effective way of learning.

There is a large amount of clip art available on CD ROM, which can be used, where appropriate, to enhance work. Most of the clip art is American, and some of it looks clichéd, but if you lack artistic ability then it's certainly worth a look. The better clip art CD ROMs come with a reduced version of all the artwork in book form which makes searching much easier.

A word of warning about clip art: you will seldom find the picture that is ideal for your purpose. You then have a choice - don't use anything or use something that is nearly what you want. If you do the latter it can change the emphasis of your work. Many teachers are concerned about the effect that computers are having on students' work in that it seems to be losing originality and individuality. Using the same clip art that is available to everyone else is one of the ways in which this is occurring.

Some CD ROMs are simply scanned versions of books. Think about whether you prefer to read it on screen or on your lap.

Clip Art from Corel Gallery

How to choose a computer

Almost all computers will do all the tasks outlined above. Most new ones come with pre-installed programs, but this is less true with older computers. Before buying a computer, it is necessary to decide what tasks you want to accomplish and then to try to find the machine that will fulfil all or most of your needs. Here are some questions to bear in mind.

1 Will it be used as a wordprocessor? If so, does it have a proper keyboard and are there suitable programs that will make it operate as a wordprocessor?
2 Can it connect to the internet or other computers?
3 Most importantly, is there a large amount of good software available which you would find useful?

There are a number of computers available which fulfil many of the above criteria. The technology changes very rapidly and new, more powerful, computers are launched regularly.

One of the main obstacles to choice when buying a computer is the fact that almost all the High Street retailers only deal in PCs, which means that they use an IBM compatible operating system. Typically these machines use Intel hardware and Microsoft software. There are other types of computers that may be better suited to your needs but you need to seek out the specialist dealers.

The thing about the new media is that you always end up using scissors.

David Hockney (artist)

For more than a decade, Apple has been the first choice of professional designers because their computers are far better designed for graphical software. Consequently, the best graphics software available is written to work on a Mac.

PCs on the other hand have been the choice of most industrial concerns, hence they are referred to as the 'industry standard'. This has led many individuals to choose PCs for home use as they fear being incompatible with the 'industry standard'. However, this is a fear that has been ruthlessly exploited to market the PC and means that you, the customer, are faced with a lack of real choice when you go shopping for a computer.

If all you want is to use a wordprocessor or a spreadsheet, you may do better to buy a machine that only does this. Boots the Chemist has a range of such machines with built-in printers at a fraction of the cost of a PC and they are portable. However these machines will not connect to the internet.

So how should you choose?

First you should decide what you are going to use your computer for. If you have a specialist need, then check out the appropriate software. Choose the computer that will run the software you wish to use.

If you are only ever going to use a wordprocessor, you should bear in mind that you do not need a Porsche to get you a hundred yards down the road to the corner shop. An old Morris Minor, or your legs, would do just as well. Wordprocessing, the most common use of computers, was just as efficient 10 or 15 years ago as it is today in that you could put printed words on a piece of paper, spelt correctly, laid out neatly and saved on disc for future reference. In this case, beware of the salesmen who try to sell you the most up-to-date, fastest computer as you will only ever make use of a fraction of its capacity.

> *Shareware or Freeware, available from magazine discs and the Net, can be a useful source of programs.*

Computers which come with pre-installed software are likely to be the most cost effective, though not all of the programs will be useful. If you want to connect to the internet you will need a modem – most computers now come with these built in.

But what about compatibility?

Compatibility is important but don't be deceived into thinking you must have a Porsche, just because your boss has one. You will fit just as well into the seat of a Mini. A lot of what is said about compatibility is just sales talk. There are several standard protocols that allow you to transfer data between different machines and different software. In word processing, for example, there is RTF or Rich Text Format while in spreadsheets there is Lotus 1-2-3 or tab delimited text. These standard formats mean you can easily move from one computer to another. Check out whether software is capable of saving and loading these standard formats. Compatibility is less of an issue with the World Wide

Web as all different computers talk to each other in the same language, so any computer with a Web Browser will perform as well as the next.

The main thing to remember is, whatever position you are in as a buyer, choose the software first.

Where to buy

You can obviously buy a new computer from a store, though what the assistants will actually know about the machines varies enormously. Buying by mail order is usually a little cheaper, but because many of these companies see themselves simply as 'box shifters' the quality of advice can vary. By phoning two or three you should be able to get the information you need, and often a better price. As always try to be wary of unscrupulous operators - some salesmen seem to have abandoned second hand cars for computers. Don't forget to increase your insurance cover if you do buy a computer.

An estimated 16% of new computer hardware is said to be 'dead on arrival', so it's important to find out beforehand about the real value of the guarantee and back-up service. Helplines are often available but are frequently jammed - before you buy from a company see if you can get through to their helpline number. For how long will you be able to use the helpline?

Before you buy, find out what will happen, and how long it will take to get service, if something goes wrong with the computer.

Beware of premium cost phone helplines. From July 1999 codes for premium rate lines are being standardised. Here are the guidelines as set out by the ICSTIS (the Telephone Services Watchdog, 0171 240 5511):
0900/1 *Up to 60p a minute. Maximum call cost of £5; fixed fee of up to £1 a call.*
0906 *Any cost per minute with no maximum call cost.*
0907 *Services with a fixed cost of more than £1 per call which includes purchase of a product eg a brochure.*

Computers

Rather like the wartime pre-fab houses, which were meant to have a life expectancy of 10 years, people are already keeping and using computers for far longer than the makers of new computers would like.

Great Computer mistakes
- *Taurus: The infamous Stock Exchange 'paperless' share settlement system, abandoned after £140m was invested.*
- *Department of Social Security: A system called Operational Strategy to computerise benefits payments was originally planned to cost £700m in the late 1980s. The government now plans to spend £2.6bn.*
- *Wessex Regional Health Authority: Scrapped a computer database in 1990 after spending £63m.*
- *Hyder: Abandoned an electricity billing project in 1996 after spending £35m.*
- *London Ambulance Service: During 1991-92 had two attempts to computerise ambulance dispatch costing £9m.*
- *Performing Rights Society: Developed a system called PROMS to computerise royalties for performing artists. So far £16m has been spent.*

Source: Computer Weekly

Second hand computers

If you can get a computer from someone trustworthy, check that it is in working order and has no viruses. This might be a good option for straightforward needs. Some dealers now sell these as reconditioned 'second user' stock, but make sure you are getting a good price for an older machine compared to the latest new model.

When buying a computer:

- get a realistic idea of what you need, and which programs you are going to use
- check computers magazines to find out about price and availability
- consult someone who knows about computers from a study angle
- try out the computer at a library, or your place of study. Some larger cities have shops and resource centres where you can buy the use of a computer for a few hours.

Don't rush into anything.

Printers

Inkjet printers are the cheapest and produce a quality almost as good as that of a laser printer. Check the price of replacement cartridges as this will be your greatest expense. It's best to buy the original manufacturer's ink as cheap refills can damage the printing heads.

Summary

The aim of using computers for study and learning is to use them as a tool - that is something which helps you to produce the work you intended to produce before you decided to use a computer. However, the computer is more than just a tool. Many people have recognised that the computer is a communication medium and as such it can have a considerable influence on the way in which we communicate. There have been reports from teachers that students using different makes of computers produce qualitatively different types of work, while other teachers say that the influence of the wordprocessor, which allows you to carefully check and change your work, has led students to being over cautious and as a result producing less adventurous work.

It is important to be aware that the use of computers can influence the type of work that is produced. If you are aware of this, then it is possible to take steps to ensure the influence is either minimised or used to your advantage. There is no general guidance on how to achieve this, rather it is for you, the student, to take control of what you are studying and how you study it. Being aware of the changes you make because you are using a computer is one small step towards that control.

FACT SHEET Working comfortably

- Find a good adjustable chair which will support your back, and let you sit upright in a comfortable way.

- A footrest avoids dangling legs which restricts your circulation.

- Some people find a wrist support useful.

- The angle on most keyboards is adjustable. Which angle suits you best?

- Avoid eye strain. Give yourself regular breaks away from the computer. While working at the computer look up frequently and focus on a distant object through the window.

 *'I use a kitchen timer to remind myself to look up every twenty minutes — I also use the break as a reminder to save my work.'*

- Avoid glare. You can check the glare on a monitor by switching it off and checking what you then see reflected in the screen. These are the sources of the glare. You can now eliminate or at least reduce any glare by:
    - moving your monitor to avoid glare from windows and lights
    - adjusting the brightness of the screen so it's neither too bright nor too dim. This is cheaper than buying an anti glare screen and just as effective.

- The top of the monitor should be at your shoulder height, and angled back about 15 degrees so that you are looking down at the screen. You should avoid putting the monitor on top of the computer as this means that you will probably be looking up at the screen which causes tension.

Does this illustration show a comfortable working position? Label the good and bad points.

' *A file full of notes is daunting so condense it into very succinct notes and headings.* '

Regular reviewing

Revision can be very demanding of your time and energy. Your enthusiasm for your subject can be stretched to the limit, but the stress can be taken out of revision by regularly reviewing your work throughout the year. Examinations set out to measure how well you can remember, understand and apply what you know. Revision aids recall, but understanding and application are continuous processes. Revision helps a student to see the course in perspective but waiting until the end of the course for this overview is clearly not the best way to study.

Regular reviewing is an efficient, effective and rewarding way to revise. Reviewing involves going over notes, essays, tests and questions at regular intervals – see pages 43-44. You are recommended to use this technique in particular to prepare yourself for examinations; it is by far the most successful method.

Regular reviewing should be built into your study timetable.

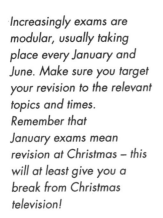

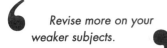

Increasingly exams are modular, usually taking place every January and June. Make sure you target your revision to the relevant topics and times. Remember that January exams mean revision at Christmas – this will at least give you a break from Christmas television!

The final preparation

There are four stages of revision for examinations:
1 Preparing your study material
2 Assessing your progress
3 Preparing a revision timetable
4 Using a variety of revision strategies

1 Preparing your study material

If you are taking examinations in June use the Christmas holiday to organise your study materials. Bring your notes up to date; your fellow students will be more willing to loan you their notes now than at any time from now on!

Check the accuracy of your notes, make sure any ideas which you don't understand are investigated. Learning is almost impossible without understanding and appreciating patterns and structure in the work. Refer to recommended books and your fellow students to help you with any sections of work you are uncertain about. In January discuss any remaining problems with your teacher or tutor.

' *Revise more on your weaker subjects.* '

Take special note of comments your teachers make about your work, see Feedback (pages 106, 108). Draw up your own feedback sheet, it is an excellent way of recording your strengths as well as weaknesses.

Summary

- **Complete** your notes
- **Correct** mistakes
- **Clarify** misconceptions
- **Check** over teachers' comments
- **Improve** weaker work

Don't listen to what your friends say about the amount of revising they've done or not done.

2 Assessing your progress

Make a fresh assessment of how well your studies are going. It is important you start your final preparations with an honest and realistic appreciation of your strengths and weaknesses as well as any hindrances which prevent effective study. Rate your progress by completing a Self Assessment Profile (page 39). Make a general comment on your progress.

RECORD SHEET

3 Preparing a revision timetable

A major part of the Easter break should be reserved for revision. About 6-8 weeks prior to exams your revision schedule should take shape. Allocate a definite part of every day for drafting revision notes (see page 140). Aim to have a full set of these notes before your course resumes. They will allow you to make the most of any revision period your tutor has set aside.

Fill in a Planner (page 19) for each week before the exam. Revision will make great demands on your free time but don't underestimate the importance of relaxation. Exercise makes a good break. Study sessions of less than 10 minutes are of little value as are those of more than one hour. A block of three hours might be broken up into 3 sessions, each lasting 40-50 minutes with a good break between sessions (see pages 31-32).

You learn best at the start and end of a study session.

Work out how many sessions you can devote to each subject and, by using your notes or the syllabus, allocate topics to study sessions. Plan to revise all topics, bearing in mind that extra time will be needed for
- special subjects/studies
- weaker subjects/topics
- regular reviewing, which is still necessary

Try to cover a variety of topics in any one block of time and avoid devoting consecutive sessions to the same subject. Alternate those topics you enjoy with those you find difficult or boring.

Revision

When you have developed your schedule, consider which strategies you should use. Make use of a variety of strategies. Review your schedule after a couple of weeks modifying any aspects if necessary. Reappraisal of your schedule and strategies can be a worthwhile exercise leading to more effective revision, but the temptation to change your plans on more than a couple of occasions should be resisted.

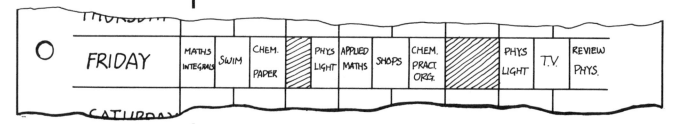

In the period immediately before exams, when you feel under most pressure to revise, avoid working long and late hours.

> Planning a revision programme makes me feel less nervous and more organised.

It is in this period that you can reap the benefits of regular reviewing and a well thought out and implemented revision plan. You should be mentally and physically fresh for the examination; a tired, anxious candidate is at an obvious disadvantage.

4 Using a variety of revision strategies

Use the range of strategies outlined below, and any others that suit you and your subject, to make your revision as interesting and effective as possible.

Making revision notes

Writing notes has helped you to understand and learn your subject. Writing revision notes will refresh your memory on details and simultaneously give you a broader picture of your studies. The notes you are redrafting will be on familiar work and an active learner will look for more details and try to understand the less obvious ideas. The familiarity of the work means revision notes can be much more concise; if you need more detail you can refer to your original notes.

Writing revision notes helps to keep your mind on the task of revising and compels you to think about what you are writing. Simply by reducing the volume of notes, you are distinguishing between important ideas and supporting detail. This selection and rejection also involves you in structuring your revision notes in order to show the links between ideas. After redrafting your notes you will have a compact aid which will be perfect for last minute revision. Before you start to redraft your notes read Making Notes, page 46, which contains a section on revising from notes. Consider writing condensed linear notes and making a pattern note of a group of related topics. Two chemistry students, for example, used two approaches to the same topic: the first chose to break up the topic and put each subsection on a record card, the second used pattern note summaries.

The aim, whichever method you use, is to make your revision notes manageable and memorable.

> *You can't revise what you don't understand.*

Using record cards

⑥ GP Ⅱ
Halides of Mg and Ca
Solubility: F⁻ insoluble ∴ high lattice energy,

⑤ GP Ⅱ
Hydroxides of Mg and Ca
$Mg(OH)_2$ not used much. $Ca(OH)_2$, slaked lime import.
$Ca CO_3 \xrightarrow{1000°} CaO + CO_2$, $CaO + H_2O$
Solubility: Both sparingly soluble, basic oxides
eg $Mg(OH)_2 + 2HCl \rightarrow MgCl_2 + 2H_2O$
$Ca(OH)_2 + 2NH_4Cl \rightarrow CaCl_2 + 2NH_3 + 2H_2O$

Uses:
i) recovery NH_3 from solvay process, ii) soil treatment
iii) Mortar , iv) Treating t. hard water, v) Paper
industry $(Ca(HSO_3)_2)$, vi) bleaching $CaO.Cl_2$ vii) Limewater

Revision

Using a pattern note

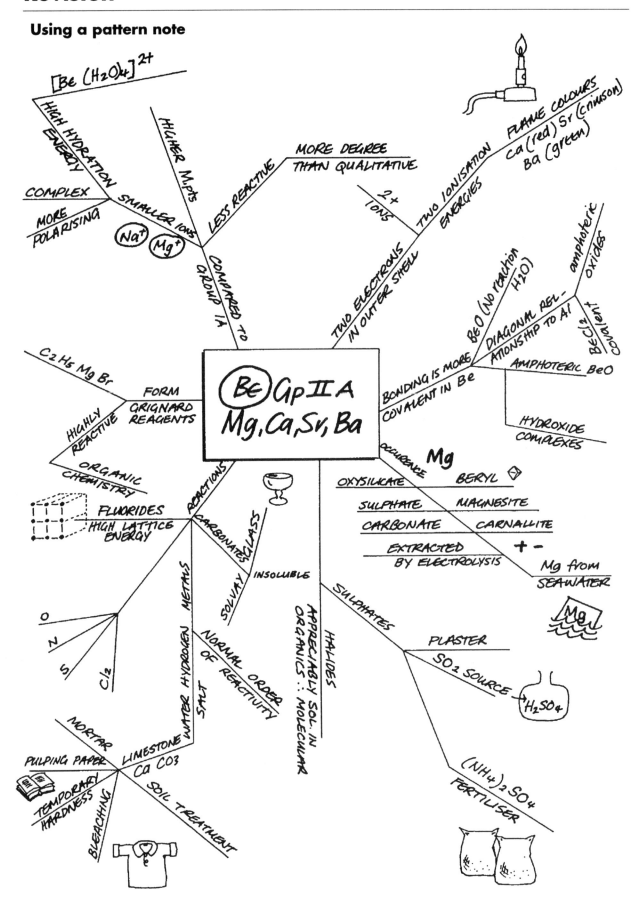

$[Be(H_2O)_4]^{2+}$

HIGH HYDRATION ENERGY

COMPLEX

MORE POLARISING

SMALLER IONS

HIGHER M.pts

Na^+ Mg^+

LESS REACTIVE

MORE DEGREE THAN QUALITATIVE

COMPARED TO GROUP 1A

$2+$ IONS

TWO IONISATION ENERGIES

TWO ELECTRONS IN OUTER SHELL

FLAME COLOURS Ca (red) Sr (crimson) Ba (green)

BeO (No reaction H_2O)

BONDING IS MORE COVALENT IN Be

DIAGONAL RELATIONSHIP TO Al

amphoteric oxides

$BeCl_2$ covalent

AMPHOTERIC BeO

HYDROXIDE COMPLEXES

Be GpⅡA Mg, Ca, Sr, Ba

C_2H_5MgBr

FORM GRIGNARD REAGENTS

HIGHLY REACTIVE

ORGANIC CHEMISTRY

FLUORIDES HIGH LATTICE ENERGY

REACTIONS

CARBONATES

SOLVAY

INSOLUBLE

GLASS

Mg

OCCURANCE

OXYSILICATE   BERYL

SULPHATE   MAGNESITE

CARBONATE   CARNALLITE

EXTRACTED BY ELECTROLYSIS

$+$ $-$

Mg from SEAWATER

Mg

O
N
S
Cl_2

METALS

HYDROGEN

WATER

SALT

NORMAL ORDER OF REACTIVITY

SULPHATES

HALIDES APPRECIABLY SOL. IN ORGANICS ∴ MOLECULAR

PLASTER

SO_2 SOURCE

H_2SO_4

MORTAR

PULPING PAPER

TEMPORARY HARDNESS

BLEACHING

LIMESTONE Ca CO_3

SOIL TREATMENT

$(NH_4)_2SO_4$ FERTILISER

Reading notes

Reading notes as a method of revision must be an active process. Passive reading can be avoided by using some of the strategies mentioned in the chapter on Reading (page 73).

You could start by setting yourself a question to answer as you read the notes. It's best if this offers a new perspective on the topic you are revising.

Try writing down the key words in a section, and when you have finished, reconstruct the main ideas using the key words. Sketch diagrams, graphs and charts on scrap paper. Mark very important details with a highlighter pen.

Using examination papers

Besides making you familiar with the type of questions which you are likely to meet, working through previous exam papers offers the opportunity to gauge how well you are learning your work. During your course you are likely to have tackled many exam questions. You probably used your notes and text books to produce your best answer, this being a good way of consolidating your learning. At revision time you should use no aids whatsoever. Prepare yourself for the question by reading your notes. Answer the question to the best of your ability. After a break, use your notes to mark your answer. Be scrupulous in dealing with every point, aim to improve it before moving on to the next question.

Some students create a bank of model or specimen answers to questions, the value of this exercise varies from subject to subject. Take care not to become too involved in question spotting if you use this method. Writing and marking exam answers will show up your strengths and weaknesses, and will help you to choose questions.

Remembering

Part of your revision programme will be devoted to remembering the factual content of your course. Testing recall only can be achieved in a few simple ways:

- answering exam questions under exam conditions
- writing out sections that have to be learned
- speaking (perhaps recording) sections which have to be learned
- asking others to question you (using your notes)
- teaching someone else. This is an excellent, but slow, way of revising
- modelling – transposing your notes from written to diagrammatic form and vice

If you have reviewed regularly, remembering will be easier

21 Exam skills

There are three key words for your approach to examinations: **plan, prepare and practise.** Previous chapters have dealt with the first two; this chapter concentrates on practising for the examination itself. Many students are let down by their lack of examination technique rather than by their lack of knowledge.

Use the sidelines to note down relevant details of **your** examinations.

The year before

Past papers

Look at past exam papers (make sure they are the right ones) to familiarise yourself with the type of questions you will be asked and the structure of the exam.

Key question words

Make sure you understand what different key question words mean:

Compare:	Are the things very alike (similar) or are there important differences? Which do you think is best? Why?
Contrast:	Look for differences.
Criticise:	Use evidence to support your opinion on the value or merit of theories, facts or views of others.
Define:	Give the meaning.
Describe:	Write in detail.
Differentiate:	Explain the difference.
Discuss:	Write about the important aspects of the topic. Are there two sides to the question? Consider the arguments for and against.
Distinguish:	Explain the difference.
Evaluate:	Judge the importance or success.
Explain:	Make clear.
Illustrate:	Give examples which make the point clear.
Interpret:	Explain the meaning in your own words, for example you may be asked to interpret a graph.
Justify:	Give reasons to support an argument or action.
Outline:	Choose the most important aspects of a topic. Ignore the minor detail.
Relate:	Show the connection between things.
State:	Write briefly the main point.
Summarise:	Bring together the main points.
Trace:	Show how something has developed from beginning to end.

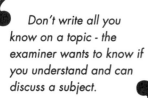

> " Do not twist the question to what you wish to write about. "

> " Don't write all you know on a topic - the examiner wants to know if you understand and can discuss a subject. "

The exam instructions (the rubric)

Find out exactly how many questions you have to answer. Are any questions compulsory? Must you answer questions from every section?

Timing

Exactly how long is the exam? Take note of the number of marks for each section, then calculate how much time you have for each question. Allow time for selecting questions, and for checking at the end of the exam. Practise answering specimen questions in the given time.

Equipment

What are you allowed to take into the exam with you?

Mock exams

The mocks allow you to discover
- weaknesses in your subject knowledge
- how effective your study skills, in particular your revision and exam technique, are
- what are your strengths and weaknesses when working under pressure

After mocks you should assess your performance honestly. See Study Profile: A self assessment, page 39.

Write down what changes you will need to make to prepare yourself for the actual exams. By giving equal attention to your teachers' comments as well as your marks, you will minimise last minute nerves and doubts.

Immediately before

The night before

Set out everything you need, such as spare pens and pencils, so as to avoid a rush in the morning.

Some students prefer to take a complete break the night before, but most people do some last minute revising. By briefly reviewing the main points in your notes you can prepare yourself mentally.

The exam day

Get to the exam room early. If you have to rush you will not be in the best frame of mind for a three hour paper.

' Don't be too calm and relaxed. Keep alert and slightly nervous. That way you should work quickly and well. '

Be concise and precise. Read the question very carefully before you start. Think carefully before you write.

Divide your time according to the number of marks for each question.

In the exam

Take a deep breath, relax your shoulders and your face. Remember you are in control.

Choosing your questions

Scan all the questions and tick any ones you could answer. Read these questions carefully - it is easy to misread titles under the pressure of the moment. Every year examiners report that thousands of candidates penalise themselves by not answering the question set or by answering an incorrect number of questions.

Planning

Underline the key words in the question to focus your attention on exactly what you are being asked.

In essay writing, ask yourself:
- does the title require an analytical or factual essay.
- does the title provide a structure for your answer.

Planning
- gives you the opportunity to demonstrate to the examiner that you can make decisions on priorities, allocating the greatest attention to the most relevant parts
- helps you to write your answer in a coherent way
- gives you confidence during the exam
- helps you to think clearly
- makes you feel calmer when you are writing
- prevents you repeating yourself, or writing too much or too little

Timing

Divide your time carefully between the number of questions you have to answer and stick to your time limits. Marks are allocated for valid points made in an answer. For some exams there is a detailed marking scheme of points which the examiners are looking for. Marks are not gained by writing at great length. The number of marks allocated to a section gives a true indication of how much is required from you. A two mark section will require a couple of key points. An eight mark section will require a thoughtfully constructed answer.

It is essential to answer the required number of questions in order to do your best in the exam. Look at the example of two students of comparable ability: Student A answers three questions at some length but has not left time even to begin question four; Student B completes the whole paper. Note the difference in their exam performance.

Question	Student A's marks	Student B's marks	Possible marks
1	15	13	25
2	14	11	25
3	12	11	25
4	0	12	25
Total	41	47	100

Writing

Many students, particularly those who haven't developed the habit of planning, go into excessive and often irrelevant detail in answering a question. The examiner needs to find a sense of direction in the essay to award marks. Too often examiners are left unsure of where they are going or when they have arrived.

Answer your best questions first but don't get carried away and try to impress the examiner with irrelevant information. There are no extra marks for answering questions which weren't set. As you write, keep referring back to the question and to your plan.

Concluding

If you wish, you can summarise your argument, but try not to repeat what you have already said. Avoid a crude concluding generalisation as if all along the question required only a single sentence answer beginning with the exam cliché "Thus it can be seen…"

If you do write a conclusion, try to save some new point for this last paragraph, or some fresh viewpoint on the question.

Presentation

- Write legibly
- Keep your work as neat as possible
- Begin your paragraphs about 5 letters in from the margin
- Number your answers (and any subsections) clearly
- Keep quotes brief and to the point. Direct quotes should be in quotation marks

It is a waste of time to write an essay in rough and then copy it out again.

Graphs, diagrams and tables should:
- be as accurate as possible
- be clearly labelled
- show their purpose

In mathematical working, the sequence of operations in an answer must be clear. Marks are awarded for logical deduction as well as for correct final answers.

Checking

Make sure errors are clearly corrected or deleted.
Rough work should be clearly crossed out.

Summary

Think then write

SIDELINES & NOTES

‘ *Think and never regurgitate facts.* ’

22 Making a video

Why make a video?

Making a video can be an excellent way of finding out and presenting information on any subject. For example, you might be studying Biology. Your teacher asks you to produce a video about the effects of Acid Rain. On the other hand, you might be doing Theatre Studies or Performing Arts; you are putting on a big show and want to attract members of the public to see it: – a promotional video to be shown at your school or college open day, or even available at your local library is a good way of raising interest.

Whatever the subject, making a video is fundamentally different from writing an essay or undertaking an individual project. Firstly, you will almost certainly be working as a team. Secondly, you will be making it with an audience in mind other than the teacher.

Before you start, ask yourself these questions:
- who am I making the video for? (In terms of audience - who do you want to watch and listen?)
- why is the video needed? (One or more of the following: entertainment, information, education, persuasion)
- how will the programme be shown? (Will it be broadcast - possibly on cable?; will it be video playback only, or large screen projection; will it be accompanied by other information?)
- where will it be shown? (On television in homes; within a specialist lecture or conference; as a "point of sale" display; in schools; available at your local library? etc.)

All of the above will begin to shape the way in which you construct your video in terms of designing the content and style to suit the audience, the context in which the tape is shown and the purpose of the programme.

Approaching a brief

First of all you need to break down the brief into tasks. This section will provide you with approaches to the research and pre-production stage of video-making. For technical assistance with production (shooting) and post-production you will need help from staff or from specialist publications. However, research and planning are the two most important and time-consuming elements of video production - and also the most important ingredients to ensure a quality programme.

You will need to examine the requirements of the brief and carry out research to determine:
- content of your video
- style appropriate to the purpose of the video, the audience and the context in which it will be shown
- production requirements (e.g. locations, experts to interview, etc.)

Finding ideas

You may have been given the subject matter for your video in the brief, but you need to come up with an innovative or catchy way of putting the information across. Ideas are rarely the product of genius alone! They are often inspired by other films, programmes, pieces of writing, adverts. For instance, imagine you have been asked to make an information video for new recruits to a particular industry (say, the Post Office) on health and safety in the workplace. Given that your audience is likely to consist of young people, mainly young men, how are you going to capture their attention, teach them something and prevent them from going to sleep? One successful way might be to use a comic genre, like the silent movie, and produce a number of scenes interspersed with captions and accompanied by piano music to communicate the salient points. Naturally, the use of 'Beware of the Dog' signs and tattered trouser legs running from the scene are a must!

Progressing an idea

Whether you are developing a factual or fiction idea, you will need to undertake various forms of research. The two main approaches are:
a) primary research, which involves, for example, talking to experts or people who have experienced an aspect of the subject you are researching; or going directly to the situation to examine it first hand for yourself; and
b) secondary research, which involves looking at existing information on the subject (books, magazines, CD Roms, news footage, off-air recorded footage, archives etc.)

Making a video

The most likely approach for you to take will be to conduct some secondary research first. Keep a clippings folder for print-outs from CD Roms, microfiche, the Internet and press cuttings. Use a system of coloured highlighter pens to identify the information that you want to use. It may be appropriate to contact a charity or pressure group for further printed information, for example, Greenpeace, World Wide Fund for Nature, or the Forestry Commission for environmental issues; Shelter for information on homelessness; the Terrence Higgins Trust for information on HIV.

(You can find most relevant addresses in *Key Organisations*, Carel Press. The thematic guide in *Key Organisations* means that you will find organisations connected with your topic that you may not previously have encountered. Check in the library for this and other directories.)

You should also take notes from books. Remember - you should always keep detailed records of the sources of your information. (See p105).

You may also decide to look through broadcast or video tape collections. Your local library may, for instance, hold some local oral history material on tape - there will almost certainly be printed or photographic archives. Perhaps you want to find footage from a particular historical period - many of the old cinema newsreels have been transferred to video. Perhaps you need wartime footage - an old black and white movie may have just the material you need.

Once you have completed your background research, you should identify the salient points and begin to work out the angle your video will take. Remember, no video can be entirely 'neutral'. You will be constructing your video with the audience and the purpose in mind. This does not necessarily mean that you will not try to present a balanced view, but a stronger video will usually take a particular standpoint (particularly in the case of campaigning or promotional videos).

The next stage is to conduct any necessary primary research. Do you need the point of view of an expert – can you visit the Forestry Commission and conduct an interview and even gather some location footage? Do you need a voice of experience - perhaps you are doing a history project - can you locate a veteran of World War 2 willing to give you eye-witness accounts of life in the war? Do you need the view of the general public on a particular issue? In this case you will conduct 'vox pops' where you interview passers-by on the street.

You should also look at any other examples of videos made for similar purposes and assess their strengths and weaknesses. You may adapt some techniques for your own use.

Finding people

If you are making a video about a particular sport, or leisure activities, local clubs and societies would be a good place to start. If you are making an 'issue-based' video, then you should turn first to the organisations you contacted for your secondary research – there may be local branches you can contact, or the head office of the organisation may put you in touch with a relevant expert who can act as a spokesperson.

You might be looking for people with very specific experiences – perhaps you are making a video on 'a day in the life of' someone with an unusual job, or unusual hobby, or someone who has lived through particular experiences, like wartime. A press release to the local paper (or, failing that, an advertisement, although this would then incur an advertising cost) describing your project and asking for people to respond is another good way to find people.

Pre-production

Once you have undertaken your content research, you will need to summarise your project in the form of an outline. An outline should be no longer than a page. It should be a synopsis and overview of the project and the stylistic approach that will be taken.

NB - Never disclose your home address in a newspaper article - ask people to reply to you c/o your school or college (making sure you have obtained permission first, of course) or to a PO Box number.

You should then move towards a more systematic and detailed description of the video and produce a treatment. Your treatment should act almost like a blueprint for your video. It should read in the running order that the video will follow and should include detailed information on content and form. Treatments take many different forms, depending on whether they are fiction, non-fiction, or are responding to a brief or call for projects from a broadcaster or other funding body. It should be no more than three or four pages (it may be only one page long if the project is a short film or advertisement). The following headings may help you to organise your treatment:

Programme: Provide the working title for your video. You may well change the title when you are nearer completion of the project, but you need to be able to identify it.

Subject/Theme: Briefly describe what the programme is about.

Audience: Who is your video for?

Duration: How long is your video?

Rationale: What is the purpose of the video – why is it worth doing?

Outline: Describe what happens and in what order.

Key elements: What you will include, e.g. interviews with experts; reminiscences; location material showing examples; laboratory experiments proving a theory and so on. (NB you should include the names of key interviewees - they are central 'characters' in documentary or factual videos).

Stylistic approach: What will your video look like – will you use voice-overs, will you let pictures tell the story, will you use particular music, will the pace be fast, slow?

FACT SHEET: Some basic terms

You want your film to be varied and interesting to watch so you should choose to use a variety of shots:

An **establishing shot** would be used to set the scene before moving on to the next shot. For example, you might use an ES of a busy street before moving on to a mid shot of the presenter.

Establishing shots are also used to show a change of scene. For instance, the outside of the Queen Vic pub, followed by interior shots, locates the action for the audience. If you wanted to change the location to somewhere completely different you would use an ES of, say, the outside of a local bank, before showing the interior.

Establishing shot (ES)

Close-up (CU)

A **close-up** is often a shot of the head and shoulders

Extreme (or Big) Close-up (ECU or BCU)

An **extreme close-up** focuses on part of the body, for example the eyes, or a shot of a wrist with a watch on it.

Medium shot (MS)

A **medium or mid shot** shows the person from the waist up.

Long shot (LS)

A **long shot** shows the whole body.

Extra long shot (ELS)

An **extra long shot** could be on a grand scale – perhaps from the top of a skyscraper across a city.

Two shot (2S)

A **two shot** focuses on two people

You specify the type of shot you are going to use on each frame of your **storyboard** (see page 154)

FACT SHEET: Placing the camera

Placing the camera in different positions can give
interesting effects. It can also affect the way the audience
perceives the subject

Often used in
interviews or
where there is a
presenter.

High level shot

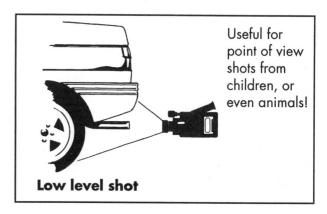

Useful for
point of view
shots from
children, or
even animals!

Low level shot

The camera
literally looks
down on the
subject. This can
make the subject
look weak and
vulnerable.

High angle shot

The camera looks
up to the subject.
This can make
the subject seem
powerful and
dominant.

Low angle shot

Camera Moves

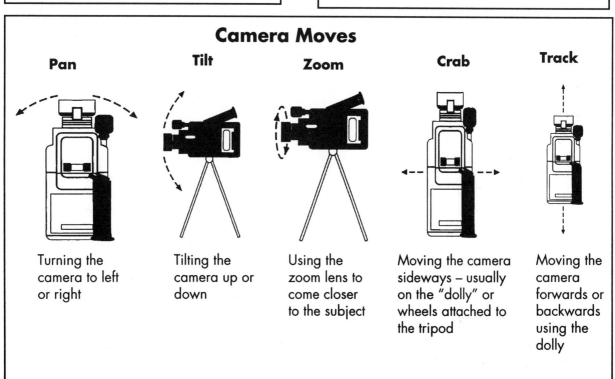

Pan

Turning the
camera to left
or right

Tilt

Tilting the
camera up or
down

Zoom

Using the
zoom lens to
come closer
to the subject

Crab

Moving the camera
sideways – usually
on the "dolly" or
wheels attached to
the tripod

Track

Moving the
camera
forwards or
backwards
using the
dolly

Making a video

SIDELINES & NOTES

Towards a script

If you are making a video in which you know in advance the precise content - for instance, you are making a promotional tape to encourage more young men to join the child care course at your college; or you are making a video to show work-in-progress on the performing arts course's forthcoming production, you may not need to conduct interviews, so your script writing can be done in advance.

If you are showing something very intricate – like a demonstration of a scientific experiment, or cake decorating techniques – or are making a video which will teach others how to do something – like changing a car wheel, or loading a camera and explaining about lenses and apertures – you will need to plan very carefully how you will show your information, and what commentary you will put with the pictures. It is advisable in such circumstances to create a storyboard (see below).

If, however, much of your programme content is to be structured by primary source material – i.e. interviews you have gathered – then you will need to shoot the interviews first, transcribe (write out in full) the content, and then select the pieces of interview you want to use with what pictures (you may use pieces of the interview with archive footage, for instance).

Storyboards

A storyboard is used in planning videos as a way of testing whether a script will work. It is essentially a visualisation of the video, planning camera angles and movements and matching shots to sound (both spoken and music or sound effects [SFX]). You sketch your ideas onto small screens, making sure that you represent as near as you can what each shot will look like (a close-up should look like a close-up – do not be tempted to draw tiny stick people in each frame!) Pages 156-7 show an example of a storyboard. Page 158 is a template for you to use.

Writing commentary

If you are writing your commentary after you have shot your footage, don't repeat word for word something that has already been said or shown on screen. Use commentary only to add to the images, to say what cannot be said by moving pictures alone. If your video relies heavily on facts, find a variety of ways of giving facts and figures, such as using diagrams or visual motifs. Visual reinforcement makes this kind of information more memorable. You may be writing voice-over, or direct-to-camera presentation, or a mixture of both. Your writing should not sound as if it is being read, but should follow the natural rhythms of the spoken voice. (See *Talking your way through an interview*, page 162, for advice on speaking naturally but clearly.)

SIDELINES & NOTES

You will need to write the commentary first, then adjust it to normal speech rhythms.

If you are adding commentary when you edit the video, you will need to time where each piece needs to be and write it to fill that gap.

Planning for interviewing

Telephone interviews

Once you have identified your interviewees, you will need to make initial contact by telephone. Remember, first impressions count, so it is a good idea to practise what you want to say - you could even write down the key points that you want to cover. You should introduce yourself by name and explain why you are calling. Check that it is convenient for the person to speak to you now, or arrange a time later. You may offer to fax the key information you are trying to find out prior to the call.

If you are only interviewing to gather information, you do not need to record the responses, you can just write them down, but you should always check that you have done this accurately, especially if you are going to quote it (Leading spokesperson for the environment, Jane Bloggs, says " blah blah...."). You can do this by simply reading back the quote, or you can write up the interview and send it to the person for checking.

A telephone interview can also be a useful way of establishing whether or not the person would be suitable to film: are they well informed, interesting, enthusiastic? Can they be easily understood? Do they have irritating speech patterns which could distract the audience or undermine the quality of information (for instance, saying "like" or "d'ya know what I'm saying" every other sentence).

Face-to-face interviews

If you are going to record an interview, you must first prepare a list of the points that you want to cover. Although you will already have done some research into the subject, you may need to do more. Consider carefully what you want from the meeting and structure it accordingly. Think of an interview as a conversation, but a conversation with a point. Ask a variety of questions - interviewees can give you facts, or they can give you an opinion on a particular topic or situation, or ask them to describe a personal experience.

You need to arrange a time, date and place. Give some indication of how long you expect the interview to take. Write to confirm why you are meeting and the arrangements. Lastly, ensure that you know how to get there. Arriving late and flustered looks unprofessional and wastes the interviewee's time.

STORYBOARD – an example

Project title:	Name:

Date

Video	CU exhaust pipes
Audio 1	Loud car noises
Audio 2	

Video	Zoom out to LS Traffic
Audio 1	Fade under SFX
Audio 2	

Video	CU presenter at monument
Audio 1	Car sounds under
Audio 2	You have only to look at the effect of

Video	MS Monument
Audio 1	Car sounds under
Audio 2	acid rain on this monument

Project title:

Name:

Date

Video	BCU detail damage
Audio 1	Loud car noises
Audio 2	To see the extent of the damage

Video	CU presenter
Audio 1	Fade under
Audio 2	caused by pollution. We conducted

Video	LS Scientist crossing lab
Audio 1	F/U lab ambient
Audio 2	laboratory tests to show how pollutants in the atmosphere

Video	CU Scientist
Audio 1	Sounds of burner etc.
Audio 2	cause chemical changes

STORYBOARD – master

Project title:	Name:

Date

Video
Audio 1
Audio 2

Video
Audio 1
Audio 2

Video
Audio 1
Audio 2

Video
Audio 1
Audio 2

Constructing interview questions

Don't ask questions that simply elicit a 'yes' or 'no' answer. You need to encourage your interviewees to reply in full sentences through the structure of your questions, especially if you want to cut the interviewer's questions out of the programme at the edit stage.

Questions starting How. . .? Who. . .? What. . .? Why. . .? When. . .? and Where. . .? will lead to an open reply, giving more than a one-word answer. You could ask them, "Tell me what happened when you heard the blast...." You could ask them, "What in your opinion will be the effect of a cut-back in public transport on the environment?" You could ask them to "Describe how you felt when you heard the news that.....". You can even direct them to begin their response to your question with the context, for instance: "The day the bomb went off in Canary Wharf, I was carrying on with my work as usual and...." rather than "I was carrying on with my work as usual and....". This will give you more room to manoeuvre at the editing stage.

Carrying out an interview – getting off to a good start

As soon as people see cameras, lights and microphones it is possible that they will go into blind panic, even if they know that you are not from the BBC! It is essential to gain the confidence of your interviewee and 'warm up' before recording begins. You could try asking them some informal questions about themselves. You may decide to try out some of the questions you have prepared. You can give them a sense of how their contributions will be used in the programme. Gain the interviewee's confidence by starting them off with factual questions - you can progress to more complex questions later.

Practise first

It is a good idea to practise your interview techniques before you go out and do it for real – you want to be as confident and appear as professional as possible! Try the following role-play in a group:
- Prepare the interview you are going to conduct – know what questions you will ask and how you will introduce yourself and the crew to the interviewee.
- One member of the group should be the interviewee. The other should be an observer, who will take notes. You should also videotape your performance.
- Conduct your interview, then play back the recording.
- Discuss the interview with your group and note down areas you need to pay more attention to. Focus on:

  whether your questions were appropriate and enabled the interviewee to respond fully

  whether you asked them clearly and in the right order

  whether you managed to make the person feel comfortable and confident in the interview

  whether you managed to avoid phrases that could be considered intrusive or aggressive

Scheduling and planning the production

Before you begin the production process, you will need to schedule carefully so that you can be sure of meeting your deadline for the project. Before you can plan any location shooting you will also need to obtain permissions to film. For instance, if you want to film passers by in the street, you would need to contact your local police to inform them of the time and duration of the shoot, and obtain clearance. Getting this in writing is a very good idea – or at least the name of the officer you spoke to on the telephone. If you want to film on public transport, you would need to clear this with the transport owners. If you want to film in a park, you will need to find out from your local authority who to obtain permission from (some parks are owned by the local authority – others are owned by the Queen!).

When you schedule the production, you need to work backwards from the deadline date, breaking down the whole process into manageable blocks with interim deadlines.

A typical schedule might look something like this:

Production:	5 minute video on Acid Rain.
Date now:	March 11th.
Deadline:	May 1st

11-20 Mar	Research (content/style etc)
20-23 Mar	Preparation of outline and treatment
23-26 Mar	Draft storyboard and script
27 Mar	Presentation to teacher/client/group
28 Mar-1 Apr	Finalise scripting. Recce locations (see opposite). Carry out risk assessment for health and safety. Book equipment. Schedule call sheets for personnel (presenter/crew/interviewees).
3-10 Apr	Production - studio and location recordings
11-14 Apr	Log recordings and prepare 'paper edit'.
15-20 Apr	Edit and sound dub.
25 April	Copies and presentation ready for deadline.

This schedule depends on having good access to equipment and the ability to shoot over a period of around three complete days. Although this is sometimes difficult to schedule into a school or college timetable, some groups regard video productions as ideal intensive integrative assignments. Such projects are carried out over a brief period of one to two weeks for production after initial research and planning has been completed. Some colleges have seen the production of video tapes as ideal work experience projects.

The recce

The 'recce' (short for 'reconnoitre') is basically a trip to the locations you will be using for your shoot. This is to ascertain their suitability and assess the production conditions (e.g. Where are the windows? Power supply? Is it too noisy? etc) and to look at potential health and safety hazards. You would need to consider:

Day/Night

Will you need lights? Will you need battery or mains lighting? (e.g. if you are filming daytime outdoors, but it is very dull).

Weather

Is there a contingency plan for bad weather?
If it is winter and cold, you will need more batteries as they lose power more quickly.

Sound

Is there interference (airport nearby, road works, motorway, wind)?

Health and Safety

Are there potential hazards for public, crew or performers?

Getting there

Is transport and access to the location straightforward? Are there toilet/refreshment facilities nearby?

You should write a report detailing all of this information to inform your schedule and the organisation of the production process.

And finally ...

Having prepared thoroughly, you are now ready for

lights, camera, action!

SIDELINES & NOTES

> *Only about a quarter of the people I see seem to have prepared for the interview.*

23 Talking your way through an interview

You speak far more words than you will ever write. We all do. Some people earn their living just by talking. They tell others what to write. The only time they pick up a pen is when they sign their names. And they are not all 'Fat Cats' or Captains of Industry. Think about a market trader who employs a part time secretary to do the paper work!

Unless you've done a lot of drama, you probably haven't given much thought to how you use your voice and speech. Now is a good time to start because what you say, and how you say it, can change your life.

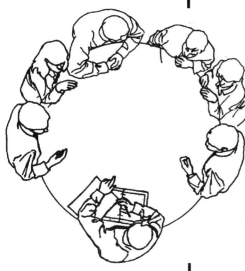

A stunning job or course application with brilliant qualifications will get you an interview. You still have to talk your way into being accepted. If you don't, another candidate with fewer qualifications, but projecting the right sort of personality, might leave you sitting on the sidelines.

The ability to stand on your feet and make a good presentation is an increasingly important part of business and commerce. Vast orders - and jobs - are won or lost like this; careers made or marred. You need to know the difference between your 'private' voice and your 'public' voice.

Knowing how to make an effective contribution to a discussion group or seminar is also important. The day might come when you are paid to go to meetings. You might be trying to sell your firm's product or services. You might be fighting for a fair deal for someone less fortunate than yourself. Either way, you need to know how to talk. You need to know the difference between being assertive and being aggressive.

But first, you have to get the job. If you are already a confident talker, don't think that you can leave everything to your sunny personality and it will all come right on the day. It won't. Like any other examination, an interview needs careful preparation.

You'll go down like a lead balloon if you don't know anything about the organisation you say you'd like to work for. Find out all you possibly can —especially people's names. (When you write, don't address anybody as 'Dear Sir/Madam.' A headteacher told me this is showing him that the applicant can't even be bothered to find out his name - or even which sex he is! That letter goes straight into the waste paper basket.)

How do you find the information? One good way is to talk to a secretary or whoever answers their telephone. They are usually happy to chat and it might get back to somebody else that you're taking this job seriously!

Next, work out what you think the job involves. It won't matter if you get some of it wrong. The important thing is to show you've thought about it.

You are then able to cope with two of the most important questions in a job interview: 'Why did you apply for this job?' and 'Why should we appoint you anyway?'

That last one won't be as direct as that. It's more likely to come out: 'What sort of person do you think is needed for this job?' or something like: 'What do you think you've got to offer to our organisation?'

Whatever you do, don't miss out here. This is your big chance. Show your knowledge of the organisation. Enthuse about it. They like that. (If you don't like what you've found out then you shouldn't be there anyway.)

SIDELINES & NOTES

> ❛ Once when I asked a candidate why she wanted the job she told me about all the things she had failed at before! ❜

This is where you try to show you are confident and assertive, but not aggressive or over confident. This is where you can show yourself as a person with a positive outlook. People would much rather work with someone who sees the glass as half full rather than half empty. It's the difference between saying: 'Five per cent of young motorists are incompetent,' and, '95 per cent of young motorists are good drivers.'

This doesn't mean employers are looking for people who can't be critical, but be careful here. Whingeing about everything you don't happen to like is altogether too easy. And it doesn't win jobs. But having strong feelings and the ability to criticise constructively can be of real value to an employer.

> ❛ I expect people to answer questions fully. Not just with a yes or no. ❜

Other questions should give you more opportunities to show you're past the stage of: 'I don't like that so it's rubbish,' and 'I like that so it's brilliant.' That's how monkeys and small children think, so don't miss any chance to show you are capable of more mature judgements such as: 'Although I **admire** him/her/them/it, I don't actually **like** him/her/them/it, because . . .'

Talking your way through an interview

We all, of course, have 'gut feelings' about things when we say: 'I like that so I'll go for it.' It's how we make some of life's best - and worst! - decisions. (Can you think of some examples?) But generally, that's not the way things happen in the professional world of work.

Making objective judgements is not a skill you can acquire overnight, so it's a good idea to start practising now. Start by making short, spoken criticisms of a book, film, TV programme, places, people, music, or a product that you know well. Imagine an interviewer has just asked: 'What do you think of . . .'

Your listeners should be able to tell you if you were criticising constructively, or simply saying: 'I know what I like.'

As well as being sure you have the right skills, an employer needs to know more about you as a person. Are you honest? Punctual and reliable? Will you be loyal? What makes you tick, and so on. It's no good them asking you these things directly because you're bound to give the 'right' answers. Instead, they use all sorts of roundabout questions.

Try to work out some good answers for these:

• How would you like to be remembered at your school/college/ university/last job?

. . . .

. . . .

. . . .

• What would you do if you found a colleague who is cheating the company?

. . . .

. . . .

. . . .

• Where do you see yourself in five years from now?

. . . .

. . . .

. . . .

. . . .

• Tell me about your faults.

. . . .

. . . .

These questions are so many and so varied that you can't have ready made answers for all of them. Try to think of each one as another opportunity to show yourself as pleasant, positive and assertive.

During all this, you need a 'public' rather than your 'private' voice. When we chat with friends, we interrupt each other, prompt and generally help each other out. Many of our sentences are never finished. At an interview, you're on your own. If you start a sentence, you've got to finish it. If you need to speak at length, pause first, think how you are going to start and, if possible, how you are going to end. Provided you know what you're talking about, the middle will look after itself.

An uninterrupted public voice needs to speak more slowly and much more clearly than we do in private conversation. Try reading this aloud:

Mairzy totes 'n' dozey totes.

Now read out this next one slowly and carefully so that its meaning is unmistakable. (In this case, 'does' means female rabbits or deer!)

Mares eat oats and does eat oats.

Can you bring the second one up to normal speed without loss of clarity and meaning? 'Normal' is slower than you think. Three words a second is about right for public speech. If you can say it twice (correctly) in eleven or twelve seconds then you're spot on. That is the pace and degree of clarity you need for public occasions.

If you find your clarity and diction simply isn't up to this, then practise reading aloud. Make sure you're not losing the ends of words – especially 't's and 'd's - or fading the ends of sentences.

If you go back to the beginning of this chapter and read it aloud, it should take you one minute to get to the end of the third paragraph. You'll probably do it too fast. If so, keep trying until it comes right.

Although this is to help you give a good account of yourself at an interview, we're not trying to fool anybody. We can all improve and polish what we are, but we cannot be what we are not. And there is no point in winning a job for which you are not suited.

Many people sell themselves short at an interview mainly because they are ill prepared and too nervous. To be slightly nervous is natural and should be expected. This can actually help you because it puts your mind on maximum alert. But if you are too nervous, your mind closes up. The cure for this is to arrive feeling properly prepared and confident that you know how to do justice to yourself.

So good luck for your next interview, be it for a course, Saturday morning job or something you've always wanted to do. If you don't get it, don't worry. Think of it as a dress rehearsal for the next one!

SIDELINES & NOTES

Summary of types of question

Leading: *suggest their own answers 'So you'll know all about the travel business from your Saturday job?' You are expected to agree and give examples of your knowledge and experience.*

Multiple: *'So what did you learn from being an au pair?' How was life different in France and what advantages can you bring to this job?' Take a deep breath and try to answer the questions in order.*

Probing: *'Can you tell me a little more about that?' These are to encourage you.*

Open: *Often beginning How, Why, Where. These are used to encourage you to speak and to show your personality.*

Hypothethical: *'What if...' Relate these to your own experiences if you can.*

24 Stress busters

A ten point plan for students facing exams

A little bit of nervousness may help your performance by generating adrenalin, but deep anxiety will inhibit you. When you are anxious you perform badly and become more anxious. You can break this vicious circle by using this ten point plan.

1 **Use** this book - the techniques put you in control.

2 **Say** nice things about yourself - be positive, tell yourself you can succeed, congratulate yourself on your successes, treat any failures as a chance to learn.

3 **Do** something else. You need to exercise, to socialise and to relax. Build a reasonable amount of this into your plans.

4 **Refuse** to be a victim. Change yourself and your circumstances. Rethink the situations that are making you anxious - for example don't think of the exams as a whole, break them down to subject level and then question level. Make the task manageable.

5 **Talk** to someone. Your friends who are also facing exams may not be the best people for this, nor may your parents. Find someone neutral and receptive - a member of staff, a counsellor, someone not directly involved in the exams. You could even just talk aloud, or to a tape recorder, then change roles and offer your own advice.

6 Get enough **sleep**. Don't study until just before bedtime, allow yourself time to turn off and wind down.

7 Make a **list**. Lists help you to organise your life and there is enormous satisfaction in ticking things off.

8 Make yourself **concentrate**. Anxiety can be very distracting. Some people use a key word or image to calm their thinking and allow them to focus on the task when they catch their minds wandering.

9 Keep a sense of **proportion**. Exams are important but you can survive even failure. There are always other options.

Read the article 'Come on, get happy' page 79

10 **Smile**. You will feel better and so will the people around you.

Confidence boosters

A ten-point plan for parents

1 **Keep your sense of proportion.** You want your child to do well, but disappointing results aren't always disastrous - there is the opportunity to re-sit, re-apply or just re-think.

2 **Bite your lip.** Don't be drawn into time-wasting arguments about trivial matters. Do be prepared to stick to your guns, or re-negotiate calmly, over important matters.

3 **Don't be a slave-driver.** Make sure they have a reasonable - but not excessive - amount of time off. Be prepared to ignore undone chores. Ask yourself whether revision or a domestic chore has the higher priority.

4 **Be positive.** Try to encourage self-belief. Avoid criticism - especially the sort that starts 'You always....' If an exam paper goes badly wrong encourage them to keep trying on the rest.

5 **Offer to help with revision.** But don't be surprised if your help is refused. If you can manage it, get your child to explain something to you (this will reveal gaps in knowledge). Ask him/her to write out a list of questions for you to ask at a later date. (Making up the questions is active revision).

6 **Practical support.** Watch their diet, and sleeping habits. Make sure that there are healthy snacks and drinks available. Don't fuss too much, you'll cause resentment and convey anxiety. Give them space and time to work.

7 **Be a Personal assistant.** Make sure you can understand the exam timetable. You need to know when and where the exams take place and what equipment is needed. Offer to get any extra stationery supplies and make sure you have spares.

8 **Listen.** Be ready to offer a shoulder to cry on or to be the target for anger but be tentative about offering advice unless it is asked for. Most advice will feel like criticism or pressure to an anxious student.

9 **Help on the day.** Make sure they leave in plenty of time, with the correct equipment, enough money for fares, lunches, phonecalls.

10 **Afterwards.** Don't expect a blow by blow account of the paper - be satisfied with a grunt. Encourage them to relax before going on to the next task. Students are usually not good judges of how they have done in an exam, persuade them not to dwell on things they can't change.

Now if he says as much as 'Good Morning', I say "Where's your revision plan?" or "Why haven't you finished your revision plan?" or "Now that you have your revision plan can't you see that you're giving too little time to maths and not enough to physics?" If he wakes up late, I say "Lucky for you it wasn't an exam day." If he stays up late, I say "I hope you don't plan to live like this in June."

Maureen Freely

More advice on coping is offered on p168 & a student's view on p169.

PASSING THE TEST

Exams can spell horror for parents as well as students.
Joanna Moorhead *learns how to avoid the agony.*

According to psychologist Dr Nicky Hayes of Huddersfield University we do our children a disservice by surrounding the business of exam-taking with a whole baggage of unhelpful myths. "The problem is our culture, and how exams are perceived," she explains. "There's nothing wrong with exams themselves - they're tools to sharper understanding and clarity. The problem is the junk that surrounds them - the feelings we pass on to our children about how exam success is somehow down to luck, and out of our control. What we should do is prepare for exams the way a runner prepares for a race: by visualising success, which every athlete knows is the key to winning. But with exams we do the opposite: we don't want to encourage our children to be confident, because we think they'll stop doing their revision."

The crucial thing, says Hayes, is giving our children confidence: confidence to succeed, and confidence to fail. "We have to sit down with them and visualise together the worst outcome - the what-happens-if-I-fail scenario. Because otherwise it's just there in the background as a deep dark pit, a terrible, awful, unexplored nightmare. You need to demystify the failure together, so your child can think - if this doesn't work out, I'll do that instead."

The belief that it's all down to chance is one of the terrors of exams, says Hayes: children are told they can't affect what will be on the paper, and that they can't be sure about whether the examiner will like what they write. "In fact you know you won't get questions that aren't on the syllabus, and your papers will go to more than one examiner." Taking chance out of the equation, she says, restores young people's confidence: so too does boosting their own belief in their ability to act effectively. "There's evidence that believing in yourself matters as much as ability, but we inherit learned helplessness from parents who didn't like exams and didn't believe they'd do well in them."

If you can give your children a feeling of control, you're giving them an essential tool for exams. "It's useful that children, even ones still at primary school, are taught time management so they become aware of the size of a task and learn how to deal with it," says Christopher Nickolls, a senior educational psychologist. "If their work seems of overwhelming magnitude, children will become anxious, unfulfilled and even depressed. They need to know what is expected of them, so they know how much work to do, when to stop, and how to feel satisfaction that they've done what's required. Youngsters who aren't given this may go on to overachieve out of desperation: they feel pressurised to succeed, but they haven't been shown the boundaries and don't know when they can feel satisfaction from what they've achieved. That's why pushy parents aren't a cliché, they're a liability. "Parents need to relax into recognising that children develop at different rates, and they also need to know that if they have anxieties about their children's performance there's a high likelihood these will permeate through and affect their children," says Nickolls.

An inability to cope with exams, and a general belief that a significant percentage will inevitably fail is, according to Nicky Hayes, a peculiarly British trait. "In other counties students are expected to achieve success, and more of them do it. It's to do with our class system and social structures - we started to challenge it in the eighties with more university places, and by making GCSEs more understandable, but what happened was more people started passing them, and because of our hang-ups about exams that worried us. And of course there are economic factors - it's more disturbing to say people aren't going to university because they can't make the grade than to say they aren't going because there isn't the money to provide enough places.

The Guardian

NO SURRENDER ON THE HOME FRONT

Daniel Walters is locked in mortal combat with his parents over exams

The Easter holidays bring not only the promise of sunshine but frayed tempers and exam pressure for many families. Exam fever sets in, with arguments, nervous breakdowns and sleepless nights. And that's just the parents. Most seem frantic to get their children to work for their GCSEs and A-levels. Bribery and confiscation of worldly possessions are just some of the measures my parents used with me. But does this really work?

In my case it didn't.

I admit I represented something of a challenge, suffering as I do from an extreme case of laziness. At the time of my GCSEs two years ago I also wallowed in a teenage "my parents are always wrong so I won't even bother listening" mindset.

Exam fever brings out the worst in everybody. My mother is an Olympic class worrier with a temperament to match. Poor old dad found himself trying to mediate between two warring factions. My philosophy on revision was to put it off as long as possible - not, I admit, a parent-friendly approach.

War inevitably broke out. It began with crisis talks, the usual lectures on how important exams are. The infamous phrase "It's for your own good", known to every teenager, became a predictable weapon in any conversation between me and my parents. The crisis escalated.

My parents, not pleased with my plan of action, decided to lean on me. Instead of the odd lecture there was constant nagging. They were no longer interested in any aspect of my life apart from how much revision I was doing. Was GCSE physics really the most important outward sign of inward grace?

Then they attempted a more direct approach. This consisted of telling me I was going to go to my room and do two hours' revision if I wanted any pocket money in the foreseeable future. That was easy. I went to my room and played computer games instead of doing my work.

Soon my parents twigged that the beeps and explosions coming from my bedroom weren't the sound of my brain cells straining over the intricacies of GCSE maths. The assault was stepped up. Objects such as my television, computer and records began to disappear. Loud and angry arguments broke out as one by one my worldly possessions disappeared.

My parents were attempting to interfere in my working schedule - or should I say my non-working schedule. And they were using sanctions to oppress my revolutionary ideals. As an independent teenager I couldn't allow myself to give in. I took my stand by refusing to work at all and arguing bitterly the whole time. My room became devoid of anything remotely interesting. I occupied myself by winding my mother up. Discussing the career opportunities of car theft and pointing out that one didn't need any qualifications for New Age travelling.

Then my dad tried bribery. Grades were allotted bank notes. I proved, however, incorruptible and by this point full of moral indignation. First, like an oppressive communist regime, they had tried deprivation therapy; now they were trying to buy me with capitalist promises. I didn't want them interfering in my life, and this to me was more important than money. If I backed down I thought they would never trust me to work on my own and always pester me.

Common household objects became deadly weapons. Chairs were broken as the shouting matches became less frequent, more intense and occasionally violent. The exams no longer lay beyond the horizon but now loomed over me.

The crunch finally came as days until examinations ticked down into single figures. I finally succumbed to logic. If I did no work I'd fail my exams. If I failed my exams I couldn't go on to do my A-levels. If I couldn't go on to do my A-levels I had to get a job and that meant really serious work. It was time for a radical rethink.

Needless to say I took a further few days to confront the text book head-on and to recover from months of neuro-dormancy. By this point my parents had given up. Regular promises of ludicrous amounts of money from my father had ceased. My mother became less hysterical.

All their attempts to make me work had failed. The end result was to make me determined to go against their wishes. Without their constant pestering I got down to some serious revision, just in time to salvage some reasonable exam results. Through my stubborn attitude and their overbearing concern for my success we had created an unpleasant few months. The next battleground will be in the run-up to my A-levels this time next year. I wonder if my parents have got the message?

Nagging, bullying and bribery all failed. On second thoughts, I could learn to live with bribery. I don't know how else I'm going to afford the sequencing program for my soundblaster card.

The Daily Telegraph

Key ways of developing effective learning skills

An action plan for colleges and schools

The ideas and strategies in this book need to be rooted into the context of the individual student's learning. Effective learning skills must not only be preached but also practised in departments and lessons.

Post 16 students rarely change ingrained study habits just because they are told they should. Advice alone is therefore of limited use. Students will, however, experiment with new techniques and approaches if

- they see their relevance to their own situation - the importance of **context**
- theory is translated into practice - the importance of **demonstration**
- they see their teachers using these methods - the importance of a **model**
- something strikes a chord eg an anecdote, a previous student's experience - the importance of a telling event/**experience**
- the motivation is strong enough - the importance of a **goal**

Underachievement is a problem caused by inappropriate learning and teaching strategies. No matter how often the curriculum is altered, this will only have a limited impact on the crucial interface between learner and teacher.

The need to raise achievement, and to meet the demands of technological development, will require learners who are able to work independently and flexibly. However advanced the technology, the teacher remains central in providing guidance, focus, monitoring, feedback and encouragement. It is the teacher who can help foster an individual student's sense of responsibility for his/her own learning. The gradual process of becoming an independent learner is central to successful study after 16.

The strategies which are explored in this book are all about the application of skills to a particular goal - enhanced learning and study. Whilst skills can be taught in isolation, there is a great deal of evidence that such skills are not then transferred to real learning situations. In other words, learning and study skills are best acquired in the actual context of the subjects the students are studying. If they are divorced from these, and tackled only on a one-off basis at the start of the course, then it's hardly surprising that students have little time or motivation to hone and practise the skills and that they also pick up the hidden message that these skills are not really valued. To sum up, learning and study skills must be part of the fabric of the curriculum. These strategies for studying are not an end in themselves but a means to more successful learning.

Staff training day

A staff training day on learning skills is a very good way of raising awareness of the issues. This can

- encourage fruitful collaboration between departments
- highlight existing good practice
- expose and help overcome any latent inertia or hostility
- release and renew staff energies and creativity

A key theme should be that rather than there being right and wrong ways of teaching and learning, there are some methods which are more effective than others, and some which are more appropriate to certain types of material. Rote learning may well be the best method for certain types of factual knowledge but it is only one weapon in the learner's armoury. It might be pointed out that a poll of employers' views on the qualities sought in new recruits put 'ability to learn' at the top. Whilst learning content is changing ever more rapidly, the subtle mix of strategies employed by successful learners can be applied widely.

As a prelude to such a day, a survey of existing study habits of the students should be undertaken using the questionnaire, p9. Staff also need to question their own learning techniques - are they successful despite poor study habits? Could they improve? Staff too could complete the questionnaire.

If it could be arranged, it would be a good idea to incorporate a teaching and learning experience on the day, for example a new software package (eg desktop publishing, spreadsheet) could be introduced to different groups by different methods. One might be plunged straight into all the details and features, another might be given an overview and asked if anyone has a need to create something using this package. For some staff it may be some time since they were faced with learning something new.

A possible outline of a day would include:

A The national context
- new qualifications & exams
- demands of further and higher education
- demands of the world of work
- implications of new technology
- tackling under-achievement

B Implications of the above for the individual school/college

C In mixed small groups for 20 minutes, each person relates a good and bad learning experience

(Why are there so many examples of the latter even in a group of successful learners?) as well as a good and bad teaching experience. Group leaders report back on common threads and most vivid examples.

D Role of the Library/Learning Resource Centre.
How can this assist both students and staff, particularly with the growing importance of resource-based learning. One librarian used The Library Game (Carel Press), with suitably adapted tasks for staff. This proved not merely fun but very illuminating. Chapter 12, Library and research skills, should be available to staff.

E Cross departmental mini lessons
Enthusiastic staff from various departments teach a mini lesson in their subject to other teachers. What are the implications for learners and teachers? What is it like being on the receiving end of a lesson? Such mini lessons usually reveal the fact that good teachers can introduce new, difficult topics, successfully by linking them to students' existing knowledge and interests. Such connections are fundamental to students taking on board new material.

F Departmental meetings to reflect on above. Report back to the whole staff on positive practical ideas to be implemented/ tried out, with a further report back after half a term.

G Plenary. Implications of the day for the real world of teaching and learning. Teachers, like learners, need time to adapt to new ways in order to feel comfortable and confident about them. Until, in fact, they become instinctive. The distinction between traditional and progressive teaching is, of course, ridiculously simplistic. Different approaches will be necessary according to the material and the students. What matters is the effectiveness of the methods and the very fact that a variety of methods is being used.

The learning environment

Consider the learning environment: pleasant, stimulating places foster learning. Students should be able to find places to learn which have an informal and relaxed atmosphere, and other places to be studious.

Such places obviously also attract potential students and parents.

The Art Department probably already looks warm and inviting. How can other areas, including corridors, become more learner friendly? Students do respond well to a more adult atmosphere, to changing displays and so on. Staff should ask themselves would they choose to learn in the existing rooms? Money is important but not the only factor here - imagination will go a long way. A tour round the building rating each area on a scale of 1 to 5 for its attractive features will highlight this issue. Visits to other educational institutions are a must!

10 Practical ways of promoting effective study strategies

1 Induction courses. Students are introduced to the variety of possible learning methods. (Chapters 2,3,4,5 & 6). Seeds are planted which can then be watered and nurtured in lessons.

2 Students are much more likely to alter their approaches to study and learning in the light of experience rather than just advice. At the very start of their courses, staff should set a task which clearly demands a range of active learning approaches. Students are most likely to try, and to adopt, new ways of working, when there is a clear and urgent need. Obviously this should be done in a purposeful, but non-threatening, way.

3 Chapters from this book are allocated to various appropriate departments so that these skills can be covered, in context, in the first term. In addition, the students should have copies of the relevant chapters.

4 At the end of their first term, students rate (anonomously) their learning experiences in their subjects. This is a high risk, high dividend strategy which obviously needs sensitive handling.

5 Tutors interview students after their first month to focus on successes and areas of concern.

6 Past students come in to discuss their learning experiences. As well as looking at methods of study, find out what inspired them.

7 Skill of the week/month - staff emphasise one skill across the board eg each assignment includes a review element; all staff conduct a check and discussion on note making; in the approach to the examinations, all staff provide the information covered in Chapter 21 or check that it has been recorded.

8 All students have a Study Planner Wall Chart (from Carel Press) to help them balance their work.

9 A session is held early on for parents & students looking at the different demands of study after 16. Chapters 2 – Study after sixteen, 6 – Wise up in lessons and 24 – Stress busters, should be used. The article 'No surrender on the home front' (page 169) should provoke some cries of recognition.

10 Staff brainstorm around these themes:
- teaching is not so much about imparting knowledge as enabling learning
- the characteristics of active and passive learning

Drama can move and influence students in a powerful way. A range of ways of using drama in this area are suggested in the next pages.

(The GNVQ 'Improving own learning and performance' provides a formal framework for flexible learning.)

Using drama

This section assumes no prior knowledge of drama methodology. No specialist facilities are required. It is based on simple, effective techniques that can capture the imagination of students. The intention is to encourage active learning, enjoy the fun that often results from it, whilst simultaneously considering some important issues relating to studying after 16.

Six clear steps are offered as a framework for creating drama. Within this, one particular drama is developed. The intention is not to be prescriptive but simply to provide an example of the way in which drama can be used to motivate and engage interest in difficult topics such as key issues in studying post-16.

Groups will respond differently to this material. The idea is to allow the group to listen to what is considered to be 'good studying practice' and for you to see and listen to what they think.

The teacher's 'script' is in italic

1 Starting a session

It is important to make a clear **contract** with the group to ask them if they feel that they would be willing to try to work in an active way. This has two purposes. Firstly it establishes that negotiation is going to play an important part in this method of learning. Secondly it highlights the responsibility you have as teacher to ensure that no one feels embarrassed during the session.

For example: *I promise I will not make you do anything you really do not feel comfortable with, on the other hand not much will happen if you don't contribute. Do you think that we could have a go at this and see what happens?*

The most worrying aspect of using drama for some students and teachers is that we will suddenly find ourselves in front of everyone else having to do something embarrassing. We need reassurance and support. In short we need **protecting in to the drama**. Negotiating the contract will already have alleviated some fears. The next pitfall to avoid is plunging the group or selected individuals straight in to a situation that they have not invested in. It is important initially to hook interest.

2 Hooking interest

Before you ask people to imagine (which is the basis of all drama) it is often wise to hook their interest. Otherwise they will perhaps be asking themselves 'why' they are pretending instead of doing 'real work'. If you capture their imagination there will be a desire to see what happens next.

Ask the group to gather around two large sheets of paper, perhaps having moved the desks to the sides of the room. Draw two blank outlines of a figure. We call each outline **a role-on-the-wall.**

We are going to look at two incredible students who have come to study here at school/college. They are both going to be stereotypes but in drama that is sometimes a good place to begin. I think it is important from the outset to make it clear that these characters are fictitious. They are going to be composites. By the end of the session we will hopefully have learned something from these two characters.

Let me tell you about the first person I would like you to help us create. S/he simply does not understand what is required of someone who has to study post-16. i.e. S/he just isn't prepared for the different type of study involved after 16. S/he is disorganised, waits till the last minute with work, panics and just hopes for good grades, complains that s/he isn't told what to do and is left just to get on with things, isn't told off even when her/his work isn't done, has got to write long essays, has got to do too much reading, there's too much pressure, finds the lessons too long.

Can you see the sort of person we are trying to create?
a *Can you think of anything else that this sort of student would or would not do?*
b *What shall we call her/him and can we think of a name that could be a boy or girl? e.g. Jo*
c *What might this character be wearing?*

Listen to responses and draw or write on the role-on-the-wall the suggestions agreed upon by the group as they come up e.g. what hair style, shoes, colour socks etc.

d *What subjects is s/he studying?*

Listen to responses and write these around the role-on-the-wall.

e *How does s/he spend his/her time? e.g. In school/college and out of it, interests, jobs, hobbies, responsibilities, family.*

Listen to responses and write these around the role-on-the-wall.

Stick the role-on-the-wall to the back of a chair and place this at the end of the horseshoe shape.

We will come back to ....(this character) in a minute.

The second person we are going to create really understands what is required and really enjoys the responsibility of post-16 study. S/he enjoys the freedom of study, reads around without being told to read specific pages, likes giving an opinion rather than being spoon fed by teachers, enjoys being analytical and thinking independently, is really interested in the work, is pleased at last to be able to write lengthy essays instead of bitty questions, welcomes spending time on fewer subjects but in depth, knows that it is important not just to learn but to understand, loves taking the initiative, is very well prepared and organised.

Repeat the steps a-e above on role-on-the-wall figure 2.

You have now created two clear characters that hopefully are far enough away from reality to be safe to look at, but close enough to be interesting.

3 Establishing the context

The reason that many students (and teachers) have felt embarrassed in drama or 'role plays' is that the context they are supposed to be acting in has not been clearly established. Establishing the context in this case simply means ensuring that all the participants know **'Who'** they are playing (**Role**), **'Where'** they are (**Situation**), **'What'** has happened just prior to the action starting (**Perspective**) and **'What'** is just about to happen (**Focus**). If all of these are clearly established there is a good chance that the drama will work. Before you ask any group to start a piece of drama, always check that the context is clear and those embarrassing, awkward moments, or fits of giggles can be avoided. If they do occur just intervene and clarify the context.

*Let's meet our first student, I would like to play him (**Role**). Let's say that s/he should have handed a piece of work in to a teacher on Monday and it is now Friday. S/he goes to see the teacher to ask for an extension – what time should we make this? (**Situation**) The teacher looks up from marking some other work. It is the student's problem, all the teacher really wants to do is get on with marking, s/he has heard all the excuses before. The student knows the teacher quite well and relates to her/him. (**Perspective**) The student goes on and on with excuses and some hints of complaints e.g. there is too much freedom, no one bothers etc....The student wants an extension (**Focus**), the teacher wants to finish the marking as s/he is going away for the weekend. S/he has given the student advice many times before without effect.*

Would someone else play the teacher?

Run the scene.

Have we learnt anything else about this student?

Write it on the role-on-the-wall 1.

4 Getting commitment

It is hard to believe in imaginary situations. If there is laughter and fun this is good and it does not stop you gently pressing for more commitment. This is a release and a necessary part of the process.

Find a partner. One person is A one is B. A you are the teacher, you want her/him to go away, B you are the student and you want to make sure the teacher understands your excuse.

You have seen one example. Maybe your scene is resolved in another way. You will not have to show these to the rest of the group. The opening line is spoken by B and it is the same as in the scene we have just done: e.g. Excuse me Miss/Sir/Name have you got a minute?...
Try to keep the scene going for two minutes. Any questions?

Run the scene in pairs.

All the A s sit on one side of the room, all the B s on the other.
A s – teachers – did you learn anything else about this student?

Write details on the role-on-the-wall 1.

How did you feel as the conversation developed?

B s – students – how did you feel as the conversation went on?

Reverse roles. A s become B s and vice versa. Same starting line, two minutes.

Split again A s and B s and ask for what was learnt and what was felt.

5 Building belief

This is what some teachers press for too quickly. With some groups this may come very quickly, with others it has to be worked for. The biggest signal comes from the teacher. If you enjoy the work and show that you think the activity is important, then you are enabling the group to take their play seriously. They will see the value in this sort of pleasurable and cheerful learning.

Let's imagine that the teacher sees some hope in our student. S/he decides to try something. If the student won't listen to the teacher perhaps s/he will listen to another student. The teacher asks a student that really has got to grips with work, Figure 2, to go and have a word with the other student, Figure 1. Let us presume this has been agreed and focus on the meeting of the two students.

Where could these two meet realistically where they would have to talk to each other for a short while?

Depending on the level of commitment you could let pairs decide upon this or select a situation from those suggested.

In pairs (same as before or change) A is the student who does not listen, B is the model student.

Arrange chairs or tables to suit the location/situation. Check that everyone is clear about the rest of the context i.e. roles, perspective, focus. Run the scene.

Split A s and B s. Get feedback.

B s, Did you make any progress?
A s did what B was saying make any sense?

Reverse roles. Repeat the procedure.

6 Reflection & evaluation

This can take place at the end of or during the session. If the students have been having fun they may not yet have realised just what they have also learnt. It is the teacher's role to help them see why, for example, there was a lot of laughter at a particular point, why particular moments may have been difficult and what the implications of some of the work may be. Drama is a group activity but the response of individuals to certain issues and problems needs to be given space. Much useful reflection can occur some time after the drama session. This presents an opportunity to re-visit and re-call some of the issues raised collectively.

Some key questions that might usefully be asked either in pairs, small groups or as a whole group are:

What have we learnt about post-16 studying from these two characters?

Did you empathise with 'the student who couldn't study'?

Do you think that a person can change their study methods, get organised and be more effective?

What can stand in the way? Is anything standing in your way?

Can you see possible ways around problems?

Think for a moment what you might have learnt, or had reinforced, or remembered, agreed with or disagreed with in this session on studying. We will just go round the circle and each person will have the opportunity to comment or just say 'pass' if they prefer not to. I will start...

Further Reading:
Bolton, G. 1992 New Perspectives on Classroom Drama, Simon & Schuster

Neelands, J. 1989 Structuring Drama Work, CUP

Owens, A. & Barber K. 1997 DramaWorks, Carel Press

Notes

Strategies for Studying © Carel Press